Jeremy Hamand was born i██████████████████████████
and writer by profession, he h██ █ grown-up daughter and
son from his first marriage and three school-age boys by his
second marriage. He lives in East London and works for an
international charity.

FATHER OVER FORTY

Becoming an older father

Jeremy Hamand

OPTIMA

An *Optima* Book

First published in the United Kingdom by Optima in 1994

Copyright © 1994 Jeremy Hamand

The moral right of the author has been asserted.

A CIP catalogue for this book
is available from the British Library

ISBN 0 356 21045 6

Typeset by M Rules
Printed and bound in Great Britain by
Clays Ltd, St Ives plc

Optima
A division of
Little, Brown and Company (UK) Limited
Brettenham House
Lancaster Place
London WC2E 7EN

CONTENTS

ACKNOWLEDGEMENTS

I would like to thank the many people who wrote or spoke to me about their experience of later fatherhood, or of being children of older fathers. Where first names only are used, their anonymity is being preserved.

INTRODUCTION

Men, unlike women, can become parents into old age and, since Biblical times, have always done so. Abraham, Jacob and Zechariah (the father of John the Baptist) are just three men from the Old and New Testaments who fathered children in their later years – in Abraham's case when he was 100.

In our own day, some elderly men who are great-grandfathers become fathers again with younger wives – sometimes to their surprise, like Zechariah. But the main concern of this book is not the exceptional, rather what is becoming increasingly common: couples postponing child-bearing until the last minute – which usually pushes the father over 40 – and men remarrying in middle age and becoming fathers all over again. Both in Britain and the United States, this represents a clearly growing trend over the last decade or two.

For the great majority of these men, older fatherhood is a rewarding and enriching experience – often more so than the first time round. For many, life can truly be said to 'begin again at 40' – or 50, or even 60 and beyond. Even when they have initial misgivings or are talked into late fatherhood by their partners, they greatly enjoy their children and find that the pleasure and satisfaction they derive from them more than outweighs the fatigue, frustrations, limitations on their leisure and the financial penalties which are part and parcel of life with growing children. Men who come to fatherhood for the first time in middle or old age do face special problems of adjustment, but few of them seem to regret the experience.

This book looks at both the enjoyment and the frustrations, as far as possible in the words of the fathers themselves, and considers how older men contemplating fatherhood can minimise any problems likely to arise. How do older men cope as fathers, especially in role-reversal situations? Is there a generation gap which makes it harder for older men to enjoy their children, especially as the children get older and become teenagers? How do older fathers deal with fears that they will die before they see their children reach maturity?

Little has been written previously about the experience of middle-aged fathering, perhaps because being older seems to make little difference to being a father: physically, most fit middle-aged men can easily cope with the demands of babies and small children. But emotionally, they are often better equipped by their experience and maturity than younger men.

Fathers today are generally different from those of a generation or two ago. Men are increasingly becoming involved in their children's day-to-day lives. Parenting is no longer seen as only a woman's job, with the father being occasionally called in to dispense discipline. Fathers today can also be warm, loving and nurturing, and involved in their children's lives in a more active way. For older men who became fathers for the first time 20 or 30 years ago and now have a second family, modern fathering seems very different – and usually more rewarding.

Older men may become fathers late in life for many

reasons. Some men do not feel able to make the commitment to a marriage and family for many years; some do not meet the right woman until they reach their forties. Some men, often with younger wives who have careers of their own, have to wait until their wife feels ready to start a family. Some men want to have a second family when they remarry in their forties or fifties. For some men choice does not come into it: fertility problems, either their own or their partner's, may delay parenthood for many years, or their wives may conceive by accident just before the menopause.

'Older' is a relative concept. Today a combination of better diet and living conditions and medical advances mean that people are more active in middle age and live for longer than their grandparents. Whereas only a generation or so ago 40 was seen as 'middle aged', today's man of 40 still feels young, with half his life ahead of him. A man who becomes a father at 40, 50 or even at 60 today, still stands a better chance of seeing his child grow up than a father of 30 a couple of centuries ago.

The 'generation gap' too may be much less of an issue than in the past. The difference between the generation brought up before and during the Second World War and the children of the 1960s seemed enormous; a generation who spent their youth in the army or in air raids, endured rationing and poverty, sometimes resented the carefree prosperous life of their children and didn't understand the social changes that were sweeping across the Western world. Today's parents – even older parents – on the other hand, are likely to be listening to the same music as their children, playing the same computer games, experimenting with fashions and sharing the same attitudes and problems.

Admittedly some older fathers will face difficulties: from the trivial, such as being mistaken in the street for the child's grandfather, to the serious, such as unemployment and ill health. But on the whole the message of the older fathers quoted in this book is clear: age should be no barrier to fatherhood, and every man should be able to experience the joys and rewards of parenting at almost any age.

This book also reflects, again largely in their own words, the experience of the children of older fathers, which is not always as positive as that of their fathers. Older fathers of the past were sometimes regarded as distant, authoritarian figures, who never developed a close relationship with their children. But perhaps those criticisms could be made of most fathers of that generation, because few of today's older fathers seem to behave in that way: they are involved with their children as much as and sometimes more than younger fathers. Role-reversal arrangements are often better suited to older fathers, who are more likely than young men to work part-time, be self-employed or be retired – although some of course are at the peak of their careers.

Just as many older fathers regret that they may not live to see their children marry or themselves have children, so their offspring often worry that their older fathers may become ill or die. But these very regrets and worries are evidence of close relationships and love.

1

Later fatherhood
in context

On average, fathers have always been older than mothers, but big age gaps were quite rare in Western societies until recently. Until about 1950, marriage and fatherhood in Britain occurred progressively earlier. On average, fathers' ages at the birth of their last child fell from 37 in 1850 to 28 in 1950 – partly as a result of smaller families. Men's ages at their first marriage and at the birth of their first child also fell.

Divorce, which had risen progressively during the nineteenth century, fell to a new low during the 1950s. Since 1950, later fathering has gradually become more common, partly because remarriage in middle age has become more frequent with easier divorce. A big increase in the number of men becoming fathers later in life has taken place over the past decade or so: the proportion of births in Britain where the father was over 40 rose from 5.4 per cent in 1980 to nearly 8 per cent 10 years later; in the United States, the proportions rose from 3.8 per cent in 1980 to 5.5 per cent in 1990.

Currently, over 50,000 children in Britain are born every year with men over 40 as their fathers. In the United States the annual figure is over 230,000. In contrast, the number of babies born to British women over the age of 40 is under 8,000 – but even this represents a considerable increase over 20 years ago.

Partly, this increase in later paternity is a reflection of the general trend to later childbearing which affects women as well as men: in both Britain and America over that period, there were relatively fewer births to both fathers and mothers in their twenties, and more to parents in their thirties and forties. Certainly the largest number of these men are in their early forties, many of them no doubt 'pushed over' the threshold of 40 by their wives' decision to have their babies later – or even at the last moment.

But most of the others are the sires of second broods which they never thought for a moment they would have when planning for the future in their twenties and thirties. Although the rate of marital breakdown has increased tremendously since the stable 1950s, so has the rate of remarriage and cohabitation of divorced partners. Many will want – or will have been persuaded – to have children in their new relationship.

Most women can continue to have babies into their early forties, but there are added risks, whereas men in theory usually remain fertile for as long as they remain potent which, notoriously, can be into old age. Apart from extreme cases, such as the American Les Colley, who fathered a child at the age of 92 (his first son was over 70 at the time), there are well-known cases of men in public life, such as Charlie Chaplin, who was well over 70 when the youngest of the eight children he had by Oona O'Neill was born.

Before the First World War it was not unusual for middle-class men to remain unmarried until middle age. An example is the case of my own maternal grandfather, who spent his early adult years working his way up in his uncle's textile firm and was a bachelor of nearly 40 when he got married in 1899. By that time he had become a director of the firm and was sufficiently prosperous to settle down in a large house outside Coventry and bring up his family there in some style. By the time my mother, his third daughter, was born in 1905, he was 45. He was in his seventies when she got married, but lived to enjoy his grandchildren, survived the air raids that flattened Coventry, and only died in his late eighties after the Second World War. Men like him no doubt were brought up to feel that, whatever the cost in sexual frustration and loneliness, it was not honourable to marry until they had reached a stage in their careers where they could afford to support their wife and family in a manner they were used to – and which reflected their own success and prosperity.

After the First World War, when a whole generation of young men was decimated, many older men who would otherwise have remained bachelors – a respectable thing to do in those days – married younger women who had lost their fiancés in the war. Today, in contrast, it is unusual for a man (unless homosexual) not to have at least lived with a woman by his mid-thirties. Sexuality is no longer regarded as a drive that must be suppressed, or gratified by resorting to prostitution, unless used for procreation: sexual and emotional involvement with another person from early adulthood is now the norm.

However, many men are 'late maturers' and are often emotionally ill-suited to monogamous relationships and fatherhood in their twenties and thirties, although women are at their peak of sexual attractiveness and fertility at this time. This sad fact of life, described by the French actor and older father Alain Delon (see page 19) as 'the great injustice', means that young women often fall in love with older men whom they view as more stable, more caring and often better lovers. They may also be attracted to their enhanced potential for being responsible and loving fathers of their children, with more emotional and often financial stability than younger men.

AGE-GAP MARRIAGE IN PERSPECTIVE

Some older husbands worry about the 'normality' of having married a younger wife, and even experience guilt at the pleasure they get from a sexual relationship with a younger woman, but in fact age-gap marriages, seen anthropologically and historically, are more the norm in many societies than marriages between partners of the same age.

In Classical Greece, men were expected to take a wife at least 10 to 12 years younger, and a large spousal age gap was nearly universal around the Mediterranean in the ancient world. In traditional societies, while early marriage for women was usually imposed to ensure maximum child-bearing and because 'a girl married young is readier to adjust to a husband than a maturer woman', men were expected to marry later. The norms of many traditional societies make allowances for the fact that men need more time to prepare for adulthood than women, and particularly where women have low status, girls are married off as young as possible to older men. This is one reason why age-gap marriages are so common today in India, Pakistan and Bangladesh, and parts of Africa.

In traditional societies such as those in West Africa, where a man marries several wives (polygyny), men were required to marry later in order to make the number of man-years available for marriage less than the number of woman-years available. Even though life expectancies are now well above earlier levels, polygyny in West Africa (admittedly on the decrease) is still supported by an age difference of over 10 years between spouses' ages at first marriage.

Fred, a Ghanaian now living in England, was born when his father was 60. An influential chieftain, his father had seven or eight wives and over 30 children. Fred's mother, who was only about 20 when Fred was born, was his father's last wife, but Fred was brought up by a senior co-wife who was more like a grandmother to him. He rarely saw his own mother, or indeed his father. Like most children in such societies, he was surrounded by female kinsfolk from birth and had little to do with his father. In these matriarchal societies, the principal male behaviour model is largely absent, with male initiation ceremonies at puberty expected to fulfil this function in the adolescent boy.

IS THE FATHER REDUNDANT?

In fact, in many societies – including our own until relatively recently – fathers had little to do with the upbringing of their children: the modern Western nuclear family is something of an aberration in this respect. Since the man's role was limited to fertilisation and, to an extent, economic support, an older father's death would hardly seem important: he could 'do it and die', like the male spider. The philosopher Bertrand Russell thought that fathers were generally unnecessary for bringing up children. In 1929 he wrote, in his famous attack on marriage: 'No doubt the ideal father is better than none, but many fathers are so far from ideal that their non-existence might be a positive advantage to children.' Modern research into father-absent families (discussed in Chapter 9) suggests that this is far from the truth, although a father's death might cause a child less damage than a violent or abusive father, and possibly less than a deserting father.

GUILT FEELING

Some thinking men who father a second brood later in life feel guilty about the number of children they have engendered. We are always being told that the earth is overcrowded and that people in rich countries use a disproportionate share of the earth's resources. So how can a man justify having a second family at all, when he has already fathered two or three children?

In fact this is, in demographic terms, a false argument, because what counts is how many children a *woman* has in her lifetime: if she didn't have them by you, the chances are she would have them by someone else. If she has already had a family, another, rather more specious argument that can be deployed is that reproduction in Western societies is currently below replacement level (that means that women on average are each having less than one daughter), and that by 2025 there may not be a large enough working population to support all the pensioners.

THE FATHER ARCHETYPE

Although historically, most fathers have been younger men, the Jungian archetype of the father is old, wise, authoritarian. Fathers in myth or fairy-tale are often portrayed as older men: God the Father, Father Time, Old Father Thames, are always depicted as old men with flowing beards. Perhaps this is because young men, whatever their other qualities, could never seriously be used to represent wisdom, and are often immature. Older men generally *are* more stable and sensible than younger men. They are less likely than uncertain younger men to copy damaging behaviour patterns from their own past. A common thread in conversations with older fathers who have had children before is how they consider themselves better fathers second time round – more involved and concerned, closer emotionally to their children. And this despite the fact that they themselves often had cold or distant fathers whom they had difficulty in relating to.

Alan, brought up in a wealthy colonial atmosphere, spent much of his childhood 'in a catatonic trance, unable to articulate or be angry with my parents'. Sent away to boarding school at an early age, Alan found his father remote and forbidding, and once grown up he rebelled against his background, living a wild life, refusing to conform and making a disastrous first marriage. Now aged 54, with three children from a happy second marriage, he seems light years away from his strange, constricting childhood. His relationship with his children is emotionally close and direct, a real father of the 1990s (see page 27).

In fact, there is a marked contrast between the experience and image of older fathers of past ages – often distant and austere figures recalled in fear by today's middle-aged offspring – and the reality of the older fathers of today, who seem to have gone down a completely different road from their forebears, and appear to derive immense pleasure and emotional satisfaction from their late broods. It is not being old which has made these fathers good fathers. They are like other modern fathers, and the interesting point is that they are not precluded by their age from being better fathers than their own fathers were – or perhaps better than they themselves were as younger men.

One striking point to come out from Brian Jackson's remarkable study of fathers (*Fatherhood*, George Allen & Unwin, 1983) was that the fathers of all ages that he interviewed 'almost always, did *not* want to be like their own father. Their childhood model of fatherhood had bred a latent or overt anti-model.' They didn't want to be authoritarian, they didn't want to be disciplinarian: they wanted to be close and present. This may have been because these men had become adult after the 1960s, a period which seems to have been a watershed in many Western societies (see' Chapter 4).

Men, and fathers, really do seem to be different today. A 1991 study found that as many as three out of ten US fathers had refused transfers or promotions that seemed likely to reduce their time with their children – a far cry from Arthur Miller's character Willy Loman in *Death of a Salesman*, who had idealised and unrealistic expectations of his sons because he had spent so much time on the road. The early industrial era's redefinition of fatherhood as little more than engendering and earning is being increasingly rejected in favour of a truer recreating of both fatherhood and motherhood.

Older fathers who have remarried may have lived in person through this whole development process. From first marriages where they were banned from the delivery room and saw little of their children when small, they have become, as older fathers, fully involved in antenatal diets and exercises, been present at the birth and fully participated with nappy-changing, getting up in the night and nursery play.

Less absorbed in their own careers, less involved in the pub life and sports fields bound up with young men's machismo, less tempted to flirt with other women, many older men put far more into fatherhood than their younger counterparts – and get more out of it. Some may have felt odd and out of place at first, but once they get into the swing of it, there's no stopping their involvement and enjoyment.

OLDER VS. YOUNGER FATHERS

Older fathers have their downside: they may be more sedentary, old fashioned and less healthy, but there seems little doubt that many older men do make better fathers than today's young men, and are certainly far less likely to abandon their children.

Young men often do not want parenthood. They aren't ready for the emotional and personal commitment and would rather not face the financial and constricting demands of having small children. For example, read this: 'Kids are just a nuisance. If I was to marry again, I wouldn't have any. My old lady wanted to have them. Only trouble was, that made me a father . . . To start with, they ruined our sex life. And they're stupid . . . It's not their fault, but you've got to admit their conversation *is* boring. And they cost money. Add that lot together and what does the father get out of it? Damn all.'

So spoke one of the young fathers interviewed by Brian Jackson ten years ago for his book on *Fatherhood*. What older father could ever speak in such terms of his children? Could any older man sound so crass, so cruel, so irresponsible?

Sociologists have written of the importance of fatherhood for helping young men to achieve emotional growth. Pregnancy, birth and mothering are turning points in women's lives: for many young women with little education and few opportunities, they are the only path to adulthood. But what about the equivalent for young men? If they have no real, continuing connection with the babies they have fathered, where is their growth into adulthood and maturity to come from? If they are unemployed as well as absent fathers, they are pretty much useless – stuck in emotional and economic infantilism.

Whereas younger men notoriously fall into fatherhood by mistake – creating pregnancies which their more mature partner may be more anxious to see through than they are – the reverse is true of older men. Some may resist the idea of a second family, thinking it will cramp their style and prosperity – and they are likely to take better care than younger men that their partner does not get pregnant by accident – but those who agree to late fatherhood embrace it wholeheartedly. According to American psychologist Jerrold Lee Shapiro, author of *The Measure of a Man*, 'Very few middle-aged men who have a child have it by accident.'

Research suggests that people really do "mellow out" between their early thirties and forties. Adults, and especially men, become far more concerned with family and relationships over these years. Even older men who have not had children before usually make better fathers, many women believe. Marilyn, married to a 46-year-old art teacher who had no children by his first marriage, thinks an older man makes a different kind of father. 'He is patient, interested, he adores our two. He is also in awe of me for having had them; he was present when they were born and is acutely aware of everything I went through. I don't think a younger man would be capable of such a feeling. Younger men walk out of a relationship and forget the children. They don't think, "I can't leave her because she had my children for me".'

What of the supposed 'mid-life crisis' and its effect on late fathers? Growing evidence suggests that the crisis simply never happens for most men, except those who are late maturers and suffer marital breakdown as a result: but that often leads to a more stable remarriage and fulfilment with a second family. National studies in the United States across age groups have found that anxiety and depression are at a low point between the ages of 35 and 60, and that the middle-aged overall feel far less exposed to stress and financial problems than younger adults.

2

Rich and famous older fathers

Ever since Charlie Chaplin, who was in his mid-fifties when he married Oona O'Neill and was over 70 when the last of her eight children was born, countless male stars of the stage and screen have become fathers later in life. Ken Russell, who had a new baby in 1993 at the age of 66, Anthony Quinn, who offended his wife of long standing when he had a love-child with his secretary at the age of 68, Rod Steiger, 68, whose fourth wife Paula, 33 years his junior, gave birth to son Michael in February 1993, Peter Hall, Mick Jagger, Peter O'Toole, Jack Nicholson, Steven Spielberg, Warren Beatty – these are just a few of them. In fact it is hard to think of many heterosexual male stars or directors over 50 who have *not* remarried a younger wife and had at least one child as an older father.

In the past, Cary Grant had his only and much-wanted daughter, Jennifer (now 28), at the age of 62, with his fourth wife Dyan Cannon. Before he died, 20 years later, Grant recognised that he wouldn't be remembered in the future through 'anything as flimsy and friable as celluloid. It will be done through the flesh and blood of my own propagation . . . Jennifer's my only ticket to eternity.'

Artists and musicians are no different: Pablo Casals and Pablo Picasso both had children late in life, Andres Segovia had a child at the age of 73. Popular composer Andrew Lloyd Webber, who has two children aged 15 and 10 from his first marriage, became an older father at the age of 45 when his third wife, Madeleine, produced a baby in 1992.

John Mortimer, the writer, who inherited four step-daughters from his first marriage to Penelope Mortimer, had two with her and then had two more daughters in his second marriage, writes movingly of the joys of late father-hood, of the preciousness of the child born in later life: 'The child of middle age so greatly loved because you can see much more clearly the time limit set on your time together.'

Businessmen like Lord White have become older fathers, as has Saudi financier Adnan Khashoggi, who recently had his seventh child in his sixties with his third wife Shahpari. Politicians manage to find time for later fatherhood too: Douglas Hurd and Nigel Lawson are just two leading British politicians who are older fathers (Cecil Parkinson, whose secretary Sarah Keays notoriously had a baby by him, hardly counts since he has never had anything to do with the child), and former prime minister of Canada, Pierre Trudeau, had a baby at the age of 71.

As one more ordinary older father, with a working wife and lumbered with child care chores and financial worries, put it: 'It's all right for them – they can afford nannies and private schools and not worry about their retirement.' But in fact these men often seem to have another motivation. When they are young and less well established, actors and directors simply cannot afford to turn down work, and if they're successful, they work extremely hard. Often, they miss out on many of the responsibilities and pleasures of fathering, and sometimes find that they and their children suffer because of this. Their relationship with their wives suffers as well – one factor in the notoriously high Hollywood divorce rate. In their prosperous later life as the pressure eases, they want to have children they can spend more time with. As most of them have remarried or live with much younger women, this rarely presents problems.

Clint Eastwood has twice been a father over 40. Alison, the second of his two children by his first wife Maggie Johnson, was born when he was 42. But he was 63 when his lover Frances Fisher had a baby in 1993. 'I always wanted one more child, but at my age the possibility had become less and less likely. Not because I couldn't have children, but because I was worried that the age gap between them and me would be so huge.' What changed his mind was Frances's insistence that he could cope with such a transformation to his lifestyle.

'Getting old has never bothered me, although I suppose a new baby will change me in some ways. But I certainly don't think that my attitude to fatherhood will be different this time around. I think I was a good father to Kyle and Alison, and I never spoiled them.'

But 20 years ago, his career was at its height and he seems to have been too busy to see very much of his two children. He never spent as much time as he wanted to with them, and admitted his fame might have damaged them when Alison, now 21, was recently treated for drink dependency. 'My profession was so time-consuming it was hard to spend the proper amount of time with them. I think it was tough for my daughter.' For Frances, 41, it was her first baby. 'At my age I wasn't sure I could have a child. But now . . . I'm the happiest woman alive,' she told the London *Daily Mail*.

Pop star Rod Stewart turned completely soppy when his young wife, model Rachel Hunter, had a daughter in 1992.

He was even singing to her as she was delivered. 'I'm besotted with her', he admitted – but apparently drew the line at changing her nappies: 'I've had three other babies to practise on and the novelty wears off', he told *Hello!* magazine.

Like his friend the late Yves Montand, Alain Delon became a father for the second time at the relatively late age of 55 in 1992. Montand, who died recently aged 70 leaving a young child, and who has had a powerful influence on Delon, described late fatherhood in an ecstatic moment as 'beyond understanding'. Delon had had a son in his thirties when married to Nathalie Barthélémy: Anthony Delon is now 28 and working as an actor in Los Angeles. Partly because of the pressures of his father's career, Anthony remained an only child. Now, in his later fifties, after years of hedonistic solitude consoled with girlfriends and Ferraris, Alain Delon has found new fulfilment in family life with his Dutch partner, Rosalie van Bremen, whom he's been with since 1987, and their baby daughter Anouchka.

Delon is tremendously enthusiastic about late fatherhood: 'It's unlike anything I've ever experienced,' he told *Paris-Match.* 'When you're 20 or 30, you're not even conscious of what it means to be a father. But when you've got more behind you than in front of you, it's a wonderful experience – to discover a new being, to witness new life.'

Although he missed being present at Anouchka's birth because of a film premiere, he now says he is totally wrapped up in his family life. 'I'm burning with impatience to see Anouchka grow up . . . It's such a paradox – this impatience, mixed with the dreadful fear of rushing the short time before she reaches maturity . . . A child turns everything upside down – and at the same time, puts everything in its place.'

Delon also puts his finger on what he calls 'the great

injustice' – the fact that most men are late maturers, who begin to become men at around the age that women reach the menopause: 'A man at 25 is a damned fool, a woman at 25 is sublime.'

Quite possibly a 'damned fool' at 25, British television personality Bruce Forsyth, who recently celebrated 50 years in show business, had three daughters by his first marriage to former actress Penny Calvert, two more by his second marriage to TV presenter Anthea Redfern, and now has a son by his third wife, Wilnelia, a former Miss World from Puerto Rico, who is 30 years Bruce's junior. His son, JJ, is now seven, and Bruce is 65, but he has always wanted boys and doesn't rule out having another one. 'We're certainly not trying to prevent it, let's put it that way.'

His age doesn't worry him. 'I don't notice my age. Wilnelia does, though. She thinks I'm too young at times! I'm like a big kid . . . I do have regrets that maybe I won't be around when JJ might really need me. But then to offset that, all that I'll be able to do for him will be an advantage.'

Comedian Les Dawson was not so lucky. He remarried after his first wife died and had a baby, Charlotte, in 1992 when he was 59. Appearing on the 'Aspel and Company' chat show in May 1993, Les commented to Michael Aspel, another older father: 'It's great having a child later on, isn't it? She's marvellous – seven months old – smashing.' Being present at the birth, he said, was 'a very moving and wonderful thing'. He went on: 'When you get to 50 you're supposed to join a cricket team and look after your allotment, and suddenly, there you are, a father – and it's great!'

Alas, Les was dead a few weeks later, struck down by a fatal heart attack while waiting for a check-up at a BUPA outpatient clinic. Baby Charlotte, only eight months old, was carried at his funeral by Les's 25-year-old son by his first marriage. The next day, the *Guardian* carried a pathetic photograph of Charlotte, bonnetted, looking over the edge of her pram after the ceremony.

Scottish actor Anton Rodgers, just turned 60, has five children ranging from Adam, 32, to Luke, seven. The last three are from his marriage to actress Elizabeth Garvie who is 35. Anton was in the news recently because of a television series 'May to December' in which he plays an eccentric widowed solicitor who marries a teacher, like his own wife, 25 years his junior. In the latest series, broadcast in 1993, they had a baby, which led to predictable jokes about him being mistaken for grandpa wheeling the pushchair, and middle-aged ladies expressing wonder at the scientific marvel of such an elderly father.

Interviewed by Libby Purves for the *Radio Times*, Anton stressed the difference between his two lots of children, although he has enjoyed them both. 'Thirty years ago I was very ambitious and all that mattered was success. I would work away from home without thinking twice about it. This time I don't. I had an offer of eleven weeks in New York, over Christmas. No chance . . . When I went on location to France for the film *Dirty Rotten Scoundrels*, the whole family came to a rented villa for the summer. I've got more time for the children now because I want it more than anything — so I take it.'

Irish actor Cyril Cusack's last performance before his death in 1993 was of Chekhov's *Three Sisters*, in which he appeared with his three daughters from his first marriage, Niamh, Sorcha and Sinead. All three were born when Cyril was in his forties, and one more, Catherine, was born later to his second wife.

DYNASTIC MOTIVES

Among the aristocracy and in dynastic families, fatherhood (and motherhood) sometimes comes late because of the need for a male heir to continue the family name or maintain the family business. Or both.

The last of the British press Barons, Vere Harmsworth, now Viscount Rothermere, owns the *Daily Mail* and other newspapers, including the London *Evening Standard*. His party-loving wife Patricia, known to gossip-writers on non-Harmsworth newspapers as 'Bubbles', had only borne him two daughters when, ten years after they were married, Vere's father Esmond, against all expectations, remarried and produced a son, half-brother for Vere, then 42.

The arrival of a new heir to her 70-year-old father-in-law spurred Patricia to try again for a boy, as a son of Vere's would succeed before Esmond's last offspring to the title – and to the ownership of the family business, Associated Newspapers. Although she had been warned by doctors that she might not survive the birth of another child, she determined to go ahead. She studied methods for pre-determining the sex of a baby and was rewarded, in December 1967, with the birth of a son and heir, Jonathan, thus making Vere, then 43, an 'older father', although not quite as old a one as Esmond.

After his wife died from an accidental overdose in 1992, Lord Rothermere spoke publicly of his gratitude to her for bearing him a son, 'and so ensuring the future of our family newspapers'.

King Hussein of Jordan, now 58, has also become an older father since he married his American-born wife Noor. With her he has had two sons, Hamzeh, now 13, and Hashem, 12, born when he was in his mid-forties, and two daughters, Iman, 10, and Rayah, seven. Hussein had several children by his earlier unions, but his Hashemite dynasty, like the Saudi royal house, can no doubt happily absorb all the sons he can produce.

3

The experience of later fatherhood

Very few older fathers regret having their children, even those who are reluctant at first to embark on late fatherhood. Most enjoy the experience of bringing up small children in middle age, or even late middle age, because they are something fresh and challenging at a time of life when things often seem to be going downhill. Careers are past their peak, age begins to slow some physical activities, new experiences are fewer and further between.

Men who married and had children in their twenties and early thirties have seen their children grow up and leave home, and have little to look forward to except retirement and grandfatherhood. The ones who remarry and set out to repeat the process of child-rearing, far from being worn out by the fatigue and emotional and financial demands put upon them, usually count themselves lucky.

Many older fathers speak of a 'deepening' of their lives, or an 'opening out', or 'loosening up', conveying a sense of recognising something new in themselves. Men whose first marriage failed because of their emotional immaturity are often tremendously fulfilled by their second marriage and feel they have been given a new lease of life. Anthony, 52, says, 'It is as though I have been given a whole second life. My friends' children are grown up and all they have to talk about is where they're going on holiday and where they're going to move to when they retire. I feel energised by everything that's going on in my life: a new marital relationship, babies, schools, the future. I have more in common with the younger fathers I meet through my wife and kids than I have with a lot of my old friends.'

Others come to fatherhood reluctantly. Larry Brill, 53, co-publisher of a New York-based magazine for older parents, *ParentAGE*, had to be talked into having a late baby by GIFT (a kind of fertility treatment – see Chapter 7). He agreed to try for a baby, but was less than wholehearted about it, and resented the intrusion on his time when the (expensive) baby eventually arrived. 'Paulette wanted the baby, not me. And that's how it was the first few months – tense and angry.' But by the time his son was seven months old, he 'loved him very much'. 'I still have my fears and anxieties. I worry about money, about the responsibility. I worry that I'm too old – too old to play with him, to run with him, to do anything with him.' Now that the baby's a year old, Larry has just about come round to the view that he would do the same thing again. 'Then I think I should stop thinking and just love and enjoy him because that's what I do anyway . . . He just said his first word: a genius! – and I'm bragging about it. Who'd have thought it? Not me!'

Many men who have had children before often say that they enjoy their second brood more. David, who remarried at the age of 45 and ten years later has three school-age boys, says that he is less involved in his career than he was 25 years ago. Like many men, he was restless and unsure of himself in his twenties and thirties. 'My second marriage is better too, and I think that makes for a better relationship with the children.'

Sometimes, men comment that they are financially better off the second time round – they are more advanced in their career, their wives earn more. Hugh Westacott, 61, whose children from his first marriage are grown up, is now a retired house-husband for his two small children. He says: 'When you are young your wildest dreams still feel within reach. You don't have the same preoccupation with the cost of children. But this time round I discussed money. I was more calculating. Luckily we could afford it. Joan is the primary breadwinner and I am much better off than I was when I was younger.'

Geoffrey, 57, remembers life with his first family in the 1960s. 'As all politicians know, people take improvements in standards of living for granted. But life for most people today *is* better than it was 30 years ago – and of course nobody earns much in the early years of his career. When retirement comes or if redundancy strikes, things may look different. But until then, life is definitely easier than it was first time round.'

Men who 'have been through it before' seem to be less upset by the arrival of small children than younger fathers. A study of the impact of children on marriage, first done in Britain but confirmed in the United States, showed that married couples are happiest before the arrival of their first child. Marital contentment tends to decrease as more children are born and grow older, reaching a nadir in the children's teens, only to rise again when everyone leaves home. However, this is not true of second marriages. Here, having children actually seems to increase happiness in most cases.

The children of second marriages often seem much more

wanted than those of the first and the parents tend to be older and more mature. While younger men often 'fall into' fatherhood unthinkingly or even by accident, very few older men have a child unintentionally. This makes for a much better relationship with both child and mother than a pregnancy which happens by default or accident and is simply allowed to continue.

Many older fathers are genuinely 'kept young' by their young children. At a time in their lives when in other respects they have achieved all they are going to achieve, when life has become easier and more relaxed, young children, with their beauty and gracefulness, their energy and their intellectual curiosity, give these men a new sense of achievement and responsibility that often seems to take years off their age.

While they see their contemporaries, with their grown-up children off their hands, slump into the slothful, sedentary existence that often comes with middle-aged prosperity, they *have* to remain lively and outward-looking to cope with the demands of young children: games in the park, swimming at the weekend, school activities. They also find they mix with younger parents and their wives' friends, which allows them less scope for the middle-aged vices of self-satisfaction and cynicism.

Often their contemporaries seem to them lazy and well-fed in comparison. The idea of having, like some of them, expensive cars, holiday cottages and frequent holidays abroad can be no more than a wistful pipe-dream for the second-time father who is faced with expensive demands from his young family in terms of housing, transport and upbringing. But most would not change their lot for anything.

Alan, a sub-editor on a London newspaper, who at 54 is

surrounded by his family of school-age children, 'can't imagine what life would be like' without them. He says they have been a stabilising influence, 'almost literally a life-saver'.

He made a disastrous first marriage, which broke up almost immediately. But there was a daughter, now aged 19 and a university student, who was four months old when his first wife left him and whom he hardly saw as a child following a bitter custody battle. Only this year has he heard from her for the first time in a letter beginning 'Dear Dad'.

He felt 'not in control' in his first marriage and subsequently 'went through a bad patch'. In retrospect he attributes his problems to his difficulty in coming to terms with his upbringing, which was stressful even by middle-class standards of the time. He was strictly brought up, with restricted choices and little physical affection. He spent his early adult life rebelling against and trying to come to terms with his upbringing; but only succeeded when he remarried and had four children in his forties. He is struck by the contrast between his own childhood and that of his own children in north London.

'If I had had them 20 years ago, I might have completely gone off the rails,' he says. 'Now, I'm more short-tempered perhaps, but also more sorted-out, and more aware of the danger of things going wrong.'

He has always liked children and been good with small children, who he thinks are 'enjoyable and fun', and was delighted to have some of his own. 'Children give life a structure and a meaning, and their vitality is a bulwark against depression and sloth. They're not holding me back, they're keeping me going!' His newspaper work, with its late starts and four-day week, enables him to take them to school every day and see more of them on his days off. 'In fact, I can't imagine what life would be like without children — I wouldn't have stuck it at the newspaper: I would have led a more unconventional life.'

Does he find it tiring? 'Yes, it's exhausting, just organising their lives. Simon is very popular and is always going to parties. Children seem to sharpen the pressures of modern life because of their acquisitiveness: one is constantly having to say no, and manipulate and organise things so that the children don't make excessive demands. We lead completely child-centred lives.'

He sees some disadvantages: 'I have a sense of narrowing options — but that is partly my age; and I spend time worrying about insurance and other things that I wouldn't even have thought of 30 years ago.'

He recognises that children are more difficult as they get older and get more control of their lives — already his older ones are becoming assertive and manipulative. 'Yes, they're difficult to cope with, but they're still admirable. I look forward to seeing them older.'

Erik Thorson, 48, a songwriter living in Nashville, Tennessee, also thinks that later fatherhood has changed his outlook on life. 'I think the difference is that in my twenties or thirties, I might have blown off my family obligations because I was trying to get ahead, whereas now I realise life is going to go on even if a song never gets cut. My career is still important to me, but I think I have a perspective now that lets me view it a little more rationally.'

Many older fathers mention the sense of renewal they feel when they have a child in middle age. A 47-year-old Denver pharmacist with a two-year-old son said he felt that having a child had put his life in order. 'It's never too late to have strong feelings about a child. It's never too late to be young enough to appreciate a child. They keep you young, but more than that, being a parent stabilises you, takes away the restlessness. You're not always looking out for things to do. Having a child at this age puts your life in order, as if, deep down, you know you've finally reached the point you always anticipated.'

A BETTER FATHER

For many older fathers, confidence in themselves and in their child-rearing ability makes older parenthood more rewarding, says John, 53: 'With my first children I was more authoritarian and also more anxious. I worried if their teeth came through late or if they seemed to be backward in walking or talking. Now I am more relaxed and realise that they do things at their own pace . . . I don't push them to achieve at school like I did the children of my first marriage.'

Tim, too, thinks that he is a better father second time around. 'Being older, we really thought through the decision to have a child, whereas first time it just sort of happened. I am more mature, I have gone through more of life's experiences, so I think I have more insight and awareness into the effects of what we're doing on the child. I have so much more patience with Max now than I did with the first ones. I didn't see so much of them – I was too involved in my career, going to conferences and staying late. Now I get to the end of the day and I just want to come home to help with bath time, read a story and see him before he goes to bed. That's really the most important thing in my day.'

Some older fathers observe that the better quality of their relationship with their second wives allows them to enjoy their children more, and makes the whole family situation more enjoyable and less stressful. Peter, 56, had two children from his first marriage, now grown up, and three in his marriage with his 18-years-younger wife. 'My first marriage was a bit of a disaster,' he says. 'I think this had an effect on the children and on my relationship with them. Because I was unhappy I was more wrapped up in myself. I feel closer to my younger children because I'm more intimate with my wife. There is a different quality to the whole marriage and that has made me a different kind of father.'

One fear which many older fathers have is that if anything happened to their wives, they would have to bring up the children on their own, despite their advancing years. (see also Chapter 9). This is a special fear of fathers who are over 60 when their children are born. Toni del Renzio, an art critic from Ramsgate, Kent, was 70 when he became the world's oldest father of test-tube quads – a contest for which there cannot be many willing contenders. But he has made the most of it, and in fact since they were six months old, he has been the sole carer during term time, while his 38-year-old wife, Doris, went back to work as a teacher.

They had tried for eight years to have a child by normal means before Doris was implanted with four of her own eggs, fertilised in vitro with her husband's sperm by Professor Robert Winston's team at the Hammersmith Hospital. To the astonishment of the doctors, all four embryos 'took'.

Can children be properly brought up by people old enough to be their grandparents? 'I have no regrets. At no time have I found any insurmountable problems.' Far from being pushed into an early grave, Toni del Renzio enjoys the challenge. He thinks he probably copes with the idiotic squabbles and demands of young children better than he would have done when he was younger. 'I am prepared to accept that they won't be as reasonable as I am.'

'In many ways, our worst problems are those that money could cure,' he told the *Sunday Times*. 'But I do enjoy life . . . Doris desperately wanted a child, and I am not sure what would have happened to our relationship if the doctors had refused treatment on the grounds of my age. I would have missed out on an awful lot of experience that I am pleased, if not proud, to have had. It has also reinforced in me a certain tolerance, or acceptance, not just of our situation but of what others might seek to do.

'Beyond being clear what one lets oneself in for, I would not want to stop anybody else in a similar position from going ahead.'

In 1993, del Renzio defended Dr Severino Antiori, the Italian gynaecologist who has been under attack for enabling a 58-year-old British woman to become pregnant. 'What's so wrong with a woman having a baby in her fifties? It's possible some couldn't cope, and doctors should certainly be cautious. But there are some young women and men who can't cope either.'

Do men who have children in their forties and fifties have trouble when they reach their sixties? Billy, a carpet-fitter now aged 65, has been married three times. His first child, a boy, was born when he was 20. A few years later, his wife ran off taking his son, aged four and a half, which caused him a lot of bitterness. His second marriage, which lasted 28 years, brought him a stepson, who was seven when he married and whom he brought up. He had no children of his own by this marriage.

From his third marriage to a younger woman, he has two sons, now eleven and eight. He feels extremely strong bonds with these boys – 'they are foremost in my life' – and have brought him 'tremendous fulfilment'. He also has two grandchildren aged 15 and 13 and two step-grandchildren, also teenagers.

Now, at normal retirement age, does he have any problems with his sons still at school? 'Not at all! I'm still working – in partnership with my stepson, who's now 50. And I'm more relaxed than I used to be. When I was young, we used to work our butts off. Now I get home at 6.30, take over the boys, help them with their homework and reading. I've had all kinds of domestic experience, but I find these kids a lot easier – perhaps it's me that's easier! My marriage is very happy, but my own son (by my first marriage) felt I shouldn't have run off with a younger woman. My stepson always supported me and I'm closer to him than to my own son. Life's funny, isn't it?!'

PROBLEMS OF ADJUSTMENT

Adjustment to the arrival of small children or stepchildren is likely to be especially difficult where a man has not had children before and is only used to the kind of life you lead without them. Rupert, 44 when the baby arrived, found his life completely transformed – and not entirely for the better. 'I had my career and was very self-confident and in control, and then suddenly this little baby came along and I wasn't in control any more. I never knew when he was going to wake up, when he was going to cry, which days my wife would be happy and which days she'd ring me at work saying she couldn't stand it and would I come home early. We couldn't go out any more, we couldn't invite friends over, my wife was constantly tired and irritable. I just hadn't anticipated what it would be like. Everything was turned completely upside-down.'

Even men who have had children in an earlier relationship may have entirely forgotten or put out of their minds all
the disruption and fatigue of parenthood. 'When you've
been for a long time with no children, then it is a terrible
shock. You're just not used to this invasion of your time
and the lack of privacy and the constant demands for trivial
things. And also I didn't realise it would be so exhausting. I
found for months on end we'd never go out and never do
anything because sleep was so precious that nothing in the
world was worth a late night.'

Most older fathers do adjust, and anyway, things slowly
get better. But some men find that rather more is expected
of them by their younger wives than had been the case with
their first families 20 years earlier. Their wives may work, if
not full-time, then often part-time, which happened less frequently in the 1960s and 1970s. A working wife has less
time for shopping and cooking and housework, so the husband has to take over some of that too. He may be expected
to get home early one or two evenings a week to put the kids
to bed because the wife has to work late. 'This means I have
a different relationship with the children – closer, yes, which
is a good thing, but I also resent it a bit,' says one second-
time-round father. 'I didn't think that at the age of 55 I'd be
spending my spare time wiping bottoms and reading *Babar*
and *Winnie the Pooh*.'

FATIGUE

Fatigue and lack of energy can be a problem for some older
fathers, but many recall being exhausted as younger fathers
too. The difference is that younger parents recover better
from sleep deprivation than most older parents. All parents

of very young children are likely to be more or less perma-
nently exhausted, but sleep experts say that people in their
forties and fifties have more trouble catching up on their
sleep and are more likely to be irritable and less alert.

Deep sleep starts to decrease with age, there are more
awakenings and sleep tends to be lighter and more frag-
mented. Perhaps this is why some older fathers are more
ready to endure broken nights than are their younger wives.
Individuals vary considerably, but older fathers may well
find it more difficult to get back to sleep once disturbed
and also to get to sleep quickly in the first place. Younger
parents score on both these counts.

As far as energy is concerned, obviously, 20-year-old
fathers are going to beat 50-year-olds in the sports' day
sprint, but older men often have considerable reserves of
stamina that younger men may not have, and older men
have often developed strategies for energy conservation.
When it comes to cricket, cycling or walking, older fathers
can usually perform with the best.

Some older fathers get blamed for not doing things that
they never have done, even when young. 'I never have liked
football and I don't intend to start liking it now,' says
Geoffrey. 'There are some things I draw the line at – and did
even when I was a young father. My father-in-law, who is
70, plays football with my eldest when he is here: the kids
know it's no use asking me.'

Older fathers' lack of energy is something that younger
wives often comment on, but the fair ones admit that it's not
always simply a question of age. Some younger wives who
blame their husband's age for many of his failings don't
realise that wives with younger husbands often make
exactly the same criticisms of their partners too. 'I remember spending a weekend with a friend's family while my

husband was away,' says Liz, 38, whose husband is 55. 'I was amazed to see that her 37-year-old husband was just as lazy as mine!'

Younger wives have to be careful not to use their husband's age in a destructive way which can be picked up by the children. 'One day when I was putting my eldest son to bed he asked me, "Why is Daddy so old? Is he going to die soon?" He's been hearing it all the time – "You boring old man, why don't you go and play football with them," "You're too old to do that," and so on. I suddenly realised what I was doing and vowed that I would be very careful what I said in front of the children from now on.'

Does the generation gap between older fathers and their adolescent children make for problems in the turbulent teenage years? Sarah, whose children are 15 and 13, thinks that it doesn't. 'It may be surprising, but I find the children respect him. Perhaps it's because he's always been much stricter with the children than I have. I think, too, that they see that he is a respected person in the outside world, somebody to whom people come for advice, and so perhaps they see him as a kind of wise old man. On the other hand, I have to cope with a lot of the problems which are off-loaded onto me because I'm closer to them and I'm there much more than he is.'

Gillian thinks the age gap does make for problems. 'He is just that much further away from them in terms of age and interests than many of the fathers I see,' she says. She also finds his relaxed attitude – one of the supposed advantages of older fathers – rather tiresome. 'He's got very laid back now that he's older and he doesn't bother with them so much. He just says, "Oh, let them get on with it, they'll grow out of it." I'm sure he's right in a way, after all, he's seen his first family go through the same thing and emerge all right the other side, but it annoys me because in practice he's putting more responsibility onto me.'

Men who come to fatherhood late in life may have special problems in adjusting to the hurly-burly of family life. Jill's father was a bachelor until the age of 40, and was 41 when she was born. He was 'too idealistic about life' and completely unprepared for the rough and tumble of a marital relationship, never mind a baby with a minor handicap. The marriage was soon over, and Jill recalls that she never knew her father in normal family circumstances: she saw him a lot, and was fond of him, but every time he saw her it was a treat or a special occasion. Had he been younger when he married, or if he had had children before, perhaps he would have adapted better to family life.

4

Older fathers as 'new men'

In a much-quoted phrase, the anthropologist Margaret Mead said that while fathers were certainly a 'biological necessity' they were essentially 'social accidents'. This was largely true of the Western fathers of her day, who were remote and authoritarian providers, rarely attempting to achieve closeness with their offspring. But recent research, both sociological and anthropological, has suggested that fathers can and often do have an important role to play in the family, and notably that the presence of a warm and caring father in the home is important for the emotional development and maturing of the children.

Related to this is the continuing debate about the 'new man' and the changing role of fathers in the family. The increase in the number of working wives – particularly those in the professional classes – has meant that women are expected to combine the roles of housewife, mother and wage-earner, and it is therefore reasonable to expect that the man should also take part in some of the household tasks and play a more prominent role in the upbringing of his children.

While by no means all modern husbands and fathers turn their hand to cooking and nappy-changing, many do, and most fathers, young or older, spend more time with their young children than the fathers of the past. One area where there has been a complete change is in closer participation in pregnancy and the birth itself. While in many cultures child-birth is something done by women with the support of their mothers, sisters and traditional birth attendants, Western countries have seen more and more a trend towards the father's involvement. British studies indicate that in 1980 over 70 per cent of births were attended by fathers in con-trast to fewer than 10 per cent of births in the 1950s, and this pattern seems to be in line with other Western European countries and the United States. Today the proportion in Britain is around 90 per cent, and many expectant fathers also attend ultrasound scans and antenatal classes as well.

The husband's presence at the birth is supposed to fulfil two functions; first, to be a comfort, encouragement and support to the mother and to express her wishes about how she wants the delivery to proceed to the midwives and doc-tors; and second, to help in the bonding process between father and child. Fathers can be involved in the birth in another way too: if things do not go to plan, the father can discuss things with the medical staff and ensure that his partner understands what is happening and is properly involved in the choice. At the point when the baby is about to be delivered, the father's excitement and involvement can help the mother through this critical stage. And while the mother is having stitches or recovering, the father can hold the new-born baby rather than leave this to strangers.

Not all fathers, however, enjoy the experience. Some feel useless, especially if the birth doesn't go to plan and the medics take over; others feel they haven't been able to provide the support the woman needs. Some fathers have been known to leave the room or faint, others are so obviously upset that the woman has to reassure them. Natural childbirth pioneer Michel Odent has been quoted as saying that he is not sure that the presence of men at the birth is natural or to be encouraged. Sometimes the support of another woman, especially one who has given birth herself, can be of much more use to the mother.

Most fathers say that being present at the birth made them aware of what the woman had gone through to bear their child and that the birth of their child was an unforgettable and moving experience. Traditionally fathers were left out of the ritual of birth; their involvement in it also provides men with a rite of passage into fatherhood.

After the birth, modern fathers are more involved too. In 1960, only 30 per cent of fathers in one British study were reported to be helping in the period after the birth compared to 77 per cent in 1980. Similarly, in 1960, only 49 per cent of fathers were reported to be getting up for the baby at night, in contrast to 87 per cent in 1980.

Many of today's older fathers had first families born in the 1960s and second families in the 1980s and 1990s and can compare the experiences. Few fathers interviewed had been present at the birth of their babies in the 1960s, and none had attended antenatal classes. All had found presence at the birth of their later children a moving and absorbing experience, which gave them a deeper relationship with their wives and also helped them relate better to the children.

'When my first child was born I was banished to an anteroom,' explained William, 55. 'The impression given was that I had no role in the birth and had to stand aside for the professionals who alone understood what was happening to my wife. I remember feeling completely redundant. My wife and the baby were kept in hospital for ten days – routine in those days – and I saw nothing of them in private till they came home, and then they seemed almost like strangers. This time I went to antenatal classes with Janet, to the ultrasound scans, and of course was present at the birth itself. Like many men, I found it quite frightening, but I wouldn't have missed it for anything – and I did actually feel I was some use to Janet during labour, and was happy to hold the baby afterwards while everyone was busy looking after Janet and cleaning up.'

Another man put it more poetically: being present at the birth of a baby born to a woman he loved 'brought me close to the vital things of life, things so fundamental that they cannot be explained.'

Fathers' involvement in the care of their small children is on the whole limited, mainly not by their own choice but because their breadwinning role keeps them out of the home during the day. A study of four-year-olds in ten countries discovered that the average daily time spent alone by fathers with their children was less than one hour, ranging from six minutes per day in Hong Kong and 12 minutes in Thailand to 54 minutes in China and 48 minutes in Finland. When the average time spent with both parents was added in, the number of hours fathers were present with their children ranged from one hour 36 minutes per day in the United States to three hours 42 minutes in Belgium. These findings suggest that even when fathers are present as an active member of a family, their direct involvement in child care can be very limited. Many older fathers may rate rather better than the average because they are likely to be less bound up with their careers, or have even taken early retirement.

While about a third of older fathers will be retired or unemployed, and others will be self-employed and able to juggle their working lives around the needs of their young families, most older fathers, especially those in their forties, will be working full-time and some may be at the peak of their careers in stressful and demanding jobs. These fathers may have to make conscious efforts to make time for their children and to find opportunities for the kind of 'quality time' which will enable their relationship to develop.

Michael, 51, is a senior partner in a West End law firm. He gets up early so as to help his two sons, Joshua, seven, and Max, five, get dressed and eat their breakfast. 'This allows Yvonne to lie in for an extra half-hour, because she works part-time and I am never home in the evenings to help the children at bedtime and I know she gets very tired.'

This half-hour in the morning is the only time Michael sees his children during the week. 'I do make sure I come home early for special occasions unless I absolutely can't make it – last year I came home to see them blow out the candles on their birthday cakes and I also took an afternoon off to see Joshua in his school play. I also try to make the parents' open evening at school once a year.'

On Saturdays Michael may have to go into the office, but makes sure he is home to put the children to bed. 'Often Yvonne goes out and I do the whole bedtime bit – games, stories, tucking them in. I also stay with them and talk to them about their friends, what they've done in the week, what's going on at school, so that I feel I am in touch with what's important in their lives. I do value the children, and certainly without them I would be much more of a workaholic.'

Sundays are kept for the whole family. 'I usually take them out to play football in the park or to the adventure playground, and often on a Sunday morning I take them swimming. Often we go out as a whole family and our outings are always things we know that they'll enjoy.'

While Michael feels very positive that he does play an active part in the boys' lives, Geoffrey is not so sure. 'As an

actor there are weeks at a time when I'm shooting some-
where else in the country or have to go abroad. In theory I
should have periods at home when I'm not working, but
I've been very lucky in my work and it just hasn't worked
out like that at all. Things tend to turn up at the last
moment so that I've promised the kids, say, that I'll be at
home at half term and we'll do something nice and then it
doesn't happen and they're disappointed. It's very, very
hard on Cindy bringing the kids up more or less alone.'

Bernard is 52 and the managing director of a toy manu-
facturing company. He has three children, Freddie, seven,
and twins of four, Poppy and Frank. Due to the recession he
is working seven days a week, trying to launch new products
and deal with the many financial and production problems
that always arise. 'In the morning I do help Samantha get
the children dressed and fed, but this morning chaos can
hardly be described as 'quality time'. Occasionally I drop
the children at school, but I never have time to talk to the
teachers or see their work at school. During the week and
weekends I get home at about seven, so I have an hour with
them before bed. Sometimes I am able to put a lot of energy
into romping, playing, reading and talking to the children,
but some evenings I am quite frankly too exhausted.

'On Fridays and Saturdays when the children don't have
to go to school the next day, I go into their room when
they're in bed and make up stories or talk about things they
are interested in, such as dinosaurs, space or whatever else
they're into. This is their special time with me which we
both look forward to.

'I do feel that I am missing out on a lot. This experience
has made me realise how important it is to have time with
the children, and I realise that I wasted a lot of weekend
time before, reading the newspaper and so on. When the

business is on a more secure footing I intend to make much more time to do things with the kids and really enjoy them. When you have a lot of time with the children it seems like a chore, but now I realise how precious it is.'

Even if today's father is not spending much more time with his children than in the past, he may be relating to his children in a different way. The father in the 1950s and 1960s probably came home from work to find the baby asleep, and his young children ready for bed and waiting for him to read them a story; he might have helped older children with homework. Today's father is much more likely to be changing nappies, bathing children and giving them their supper.

If today's fathers are different, when did the great change occur and why? Clearly the answer varies with different societies, different classes and different families; but it does seem clear that the 1960s represented some kind of watershed in personal and social attitudes in most Western societies. Dissatisfaction with old values, advances in medicine and psychiatry, easier divorce, the explosion of popular music, the widespread availability of 'soft' drugs, perhaps above all the arrival of the contraceptive pill – these and other factors coalesced to wreak a transformation in family values and family formation. The term 'generation gap' was first heard in the 1960s and it was indeed a reality at that time: the adolescents of the 1960s had parents who were adolescents before or during the Second World War – and the gap was probably bigger than it has ever been before or since. By the same token, parents who were young adults in the 1960s – and that includes most of today's older fathers – are not so remote from today's generation of young people as they were from their own fathers.

There was certainly a major transformation in attitudes and often lifestyles between the fathers of the 1950s and the fathers of the 1970s and after. A study in the UK in 1979 showed that only 5 per cent of first- and second-time fathers did not participate in the care of their one-year-olds. Twenty years earlier the proportion of fathers who provided no help was 70 per cent.

Studies of the US media have found that the pre-1970 depiction of fathers was of bumbling, ineffectual individuals. Today this has changed to reflect the important role that fathers take in the social and emotional development of their children, and a number of Hollywood films, such as *Kramer v. Kramer*, have even dealt positively with the issue of single fathers.

Does the fact that modern fathers do more caring for their children change the relationship between father and child? James thinks that it does. 'The old idea of the father – the image I had of my own – was a rather remote figure, the one who laid down the law, told us off, although he would sometimes take part in sports and other games. I spend far more time caring for my son, he is much more likely to come to me for comfort if he has hurt himself or to ask me to help him with things.'

The change in parenting roles has created some difficulties for couples in adjusting to the new baby. In the old days the roles were clear; the man was the breadwinner and disciplinarian, the mother looked after the children and was their comforter. But fatherhood is no longer confined to finance. Male unemployment and female employment mean that many families have two breadwinners. In the traditional psychoanalytic view, the father is the child's connection with the outside world. But often the mother is now fulfilling part of that function. In return, many men are asking that there should be a closer emotional and nurturing connection between children and fathers.

When women work and fathers take more care of the children, conflicts can arise. Couples find they are arguing about who has changed the most nappies and whose turn it is to feed the baby. As the child gets older he finds he can play one parent off against the other and get double doses of attention.

When a baby is finally born to a couple who have been married or living together for a long time, the impact on their relationship can be considerable. 'We had a lot of adjusting to do, and we didn't do it very well,' recalls Tim, who had been married to Liz for ten years before they had their first child at the ages of 43 and 39 respectively. 'We were both used to being in control of everything, and then suddenly there was this screaming person who had to have everything done instantly. Gone were our evenings out, Sunday morning lie-ins, entertaining friends for dinner and going away for romantic weekends. We were stuck together in the house and fighting over whose turn it was to hold the baby.'

When both partners work the stresses of a child can be enormous. 'We would plan every week, who would be available when to take the child to the childminders or collect him, who could baby-sit one night when the other had to go to some work-related function, what to do when I was away for a conference or when she had to work late. Neither of us could spontaneously do anything; everything had to be pre-planned and pre-arranged. If either of us was ill this upset all the arrangements and instead of showing sympathy we would be angry and fed up.'

Most older fathers whose wives worked felt that the wife made a lot of demands. Tim's wife worked part-time as a journalist and her job was demanding and sometimes erratic, and while useful to supplement the family income, brought in much less than his job in the City. 'I understand that her job is important, but when things clash she just doesn't seem to understand that I am the main breadwinner and I can't just skip home to look after Joe because she has a meeting that's running late.'

The kinds of arguments that can arise when both father and mother are working can seem unbelievably petty, but they hurt. 'When Joe woke in the night we were arguing about whose turn it was to go to him. Was it mine because she's been with him all day or hers because I got up last night? Unless you keep a chart of every nappy change and every time you take the child for a walk so the other person can get on with something, you're never going to get it right and even then you wouldn't manage it. It's just we're both so tired and stressed all the time we're constantly trying to dump everything on the other person.'

Jo, who had a daughter by her older husband, says that she feels she bears the brunt of parenting. 'First, this was because he had had two children before and I think it was always understood that this was 'my' baby. I found there were fewer arguments if I just got on and did it all so I didn't complain. There was a stage when Amy wouldn't go to him very readily because she just wasn't used to being with him and I did point out to him what was happening and that in the end he'd lose out. He is quite good with her now, he plays games and doesn't ask a lot. I think that's one area in which older fathers score; they are much more accepting of what people are, he's not always pushing her or wanting her to be what she's not as some younger fathers seem to be.'

A common criticism of fathers of the past – perhaps

especially older fathers of the past – was that they were
'cold' and 'remote'. It is a criticism seldom heard today of
fathers young or old. This is surely because closer involvement with their children, which is now the social norm, is
actually very rewarding and allows men to express emo-
tions not otherwise encouraged by society. Certainly, as
the recent UNESCO book *Families* asserts, 'Men who miss
out on the nurturing role within a family miss some of the
greatest joys in life.'

'ROLE REVERSAL'

Some older fathers quite happily become 'house-husbands'
and take over virtually the whole of the nurturing of their
small children to enable their wives to pursue their careers.
In the United States, there is even a magazine, *Full-Time
Dads*, featuring the joys and pleasures of nurturing small
children, to cater for the considerable number of men who
are home-bound house-husbands. It may well be that older
fathers are less likely than younger men to have problems
with role reversal because, if not retired, they may have
moved on to part-time working or self-employment, or at
any rate no longer have any career ambitions to satisfy.

Researchers have pointed out that even where fathers
have the main responsibility for child care, they do not necessarily assume the overall responsibility for children in the
way that traditional mothers do. Many mothers retain
greater responsibility for decision-making, planning,
monitoring and anticipating the needs of the children, and
'take over' when they get home from work.

Few fathers are able to anticipate the difficulties they will
experience in staying at home and caring for children –

although 'second-time-round' older fathers may be more realistic. Although many look upon their new job with enthusiasm and have expectations about achieving things while at home (such as redecorating, starting a new hobby, or writing a book), most are forced to revise their attitudes. In one recent study of reversed-role fathers, nearly 60 per cent reported difficulties in adjusting to the demands of child care and housework, complaining about the relentlessness of the task, the boredom, the physical work involved and the lack of adult company. Seventy-four per cent of the mothers also reported that their partners experienced such difficulties. As would be expected, fathers who felt they had been forced to reverse roles reported more problems than those who had chosen to.

Raymond Thompson describes himself as a 'refurbished man' rather than a 'new man', because of his grey hair and middle-age spread. He had two children by his first marriage, 'but I have to admit that the difficulties of building a career meant I didn't spend as much time with them as I would have liked to.' When he remarried he didn't expect to have any more, but when his daughter was born he was overcome by unexpected paternal instincts, and instead of employing a nanny to allow his wife to resume her high-flying legal career, Raymond decided to run his legal practice from home and combine work with paternity.

Despite careful planning, he soon struck problems: 'Full-time fatherhood cannot be run in the same way as my business.' And clients speaking to him on the telephone were disconcerted by vocal demands for food or attention. Eight months after he started his new life, his work tends to get done at weekends and at night, or when the baby is asleep. 'I've become a dab hand at operating the computer one-handed while bottle-feeding with the other.'

His wife admitted to feeling she was missing out on things, but they have persevered and she makes a concerted effort to spend as much time with their child as possible. Meanwhile, in order to do some of the things that are important to him, Raymond has even lashed the carry-cot to a golf buggy takes his daughter round 18 holes. 'I have little time to work and can never understand how other parents' houses are so tidy,' he told the *Daily Telegraph*. 'My golf handicap has rocketed, my profits have slumped, I sleep when I can and I feel ten years older. But I was the first to get one of Emily's flashing smiles, she's terrific company, and she keeps me amused for hours.'

An unusual role-reversal dad is the British art critic Toni del Renzio who became a father of quads at the age of 70 (see page 31) and has been prime carer, during the school holidays, of his children, now aged eight, since they were six months old.

Hugh Westacott (see page 26) married his second wife, then aged 33, after a ten-day romance, at the age of 53. When they had children, he took early retirement from local government and looked after the children while Joan, an American librarian, worked full-time. They now have two children, aged five and two, and he has cared for both of them more or less full-time since they were three months old. In each case, as soon as Joan's maternity leave came to an end, he took over total daytime care, including feeding with expressed breast milk until they were 10 months old.

'It's true that I have seen more of the children than Joan! It's been wonderful – why do women want to go back to work?' he muses. Although retired from his full-time job, he has a secondary career as a freelance journalist, writing about rambling, cycling and other outdoor pursuits. Joan takes over the children at the weekend, so he has all day

Saturday for his journalism, and also usually stays behind and works when Joan takes the children to visit her family in Texas during the school holidays.

Looking back at his first-time fatherhood in his thirties – he has two daughters now aged 28 and 25 – he feels he is more tolerant of the foibles of small children than he was then, and more resistant to broken nights. Like other older fathers, he thinks he is less anxious than his younger wife about the children's illnesses and is not alarmed when they develop temperatures or earaches. 'I accept that they are going to have minor ailments and get far less upset about it than Joan sometimes does,' he says.

The idea of being a house-father while his wife works has never worried him and he has never been embarrassed about 'what people think'. He says he is not a man's man, despises macho culture and has always mainly worked with women.

'I wouldn't have missed these years for anything,' he says with feeling. On the down side, he is less tolerant of noise than he was when was young, and the baby is very noisy. One of the few problems he has had was when he wanted to take his little son to a mother-and-toddler playgroup. 'The wariness and even hostility of the mothers really shocked me. Women are always banging on about men taking a more active role in child care, but when it actually happens, they seem to resent it.'

Incredibly, some of the mothers seemed to be afraid of him as a potential molester: when he picked up one little girl who had fallen over and was crying, the mother flew at him, screaming, 'Don't you ever dare touch my daughter again!' Eventually, he took three or four mothers home for tea and explained that he found their attitude strange and hurtful. That cleared the air a bit and things improved.

Such attitudes are by no means unusual: widowed and

single fathers caring for small children often report similar hostility towards them from groups of mothers, who obviously find difficulty in accepting men into their circle. Charles, whose wife tragically died soon after their baby was born, attempted to attend a mother-and-baby group with some of the mothers who had attended the same antenatal classes as he and his wife. After a few weeks they asked him not to come because they felt embarrassed having their usual conversations and breast feeding in front of a man.

Some fathers on the other hand find developing close supportive networks with women in the neighbourhood a problem because of the threat they see this as having on marital relationships. For these and other reasons, fathers at home become even more socially isolated than women at home, and this is often a reason for families failing to maintain the role-reversal lifestyle.

In fact, many role-reversed fathers revert to traditional arrangements after a few years, sometimes because unemployed fathers get another job, sometimes because of dissatisfaction or disappointment. But older fathers are usually more able to cope with the situation and are less likely to want, or be able, to go back to full-time employment. Another factor is the dissatisfaction of mothers, who find their lifestyle in full employment too demanding and miss spending time with their children. Also, although a lot is said about men feeling threatened by women changing roles, very little is said about women feeling threatened by men wanting to share more in child care.

Some mothers certainly do find difficulty in accepting their spouse in his 'domestic role', and their children becoming more attached to their father and going to him when they need comfort and support. Some suggest that their spouse's standards of child care are not as high as theirs –

especially that the father is 'too soft' with the children. Most of all, some wives resent the status and credit that other people (and especially other women) give their spouses because of their involvement in child care. The comment they resented most was: 'Oh, isn't he marvellous!' They, after all, had been child-carers before and no one had suggested that they were marvellous.

'The feminist message to men has been taken on board,' says Dr Arlene Vetere, clinical psychologist and lecturer at Reading University. 'But it may rebound: 'new' men are now taking over much of the emotional, caring role from women, and women are not always happy about this. We'll see more of this.'

Dr Vetere believes that contemporary men's increasing emotional involvement with their children is an important social phenomenon. 'Research suggests that the "mid-life crisis", although supposedly about *people*, is really about *men*, not women. It is men who re-evaluate their career in middle age or rethink their career emphasis. In this process of re-prioritising, relationships often come off much better. Men who have construed themselves as wage-earners reach crisis point, realising they have lost out.'

Sometimes the trigger is aggressive behaviour by adolescent children, leading to an acute sense of failure in their father. For many men, it is a painful adjustment; sometimes it is a factor in divorce when the men come to realise that their relationship with their wives has suffered because they have cut themselves off from full emotional involvement with their families. Unfortunately there is often no turning back: the obvious way forward being a new relationship – and, perhaps, new children.

EXPLOITATION

Are older role-reversal fathers more likely to be 'put upon' by career-conscious wives? Some may give this impression because the fact that they are retired or self-employed enables them to spend more time with the children and do more domestic chores. Friends and colleagues may think that older fathers are exploited, but this seems rarely to be the case in reality, and the idea probably derives from ingrained social prejudice rather than from what has happened to the fathers themselves.

For although the equality of the sexes in public and private life is accepted in principle today, our society still has some way to go to assimilate the *practice* of gender equality, and the sight of an older father pushing a pushchair, changing nappies or even doing the shopping may cause conservative eyebrows to twitch.

Obviously, more older fathers than younger fathers are likely to be in role-reversal households, but this doesn't mean they are being exploited, willingly or otherwise. Even if there are cases, they are hugely outnumbered by the number of women exploited in more 'traditional' relationships. Research has shown that the female partners in dual-income households are often exploited because they are expected to do the lion's share of housework, cooking and child care as well as holding down a full-time job. Sometimes it is the children who are exploited by mothers or fathers who are too bound up in their careers to spend enough time with them. This accusation can often be made of younger fathers, but more rarely of older fathers.

Prudence is a barrister who first married at the age of 40 an older man she had met through the local political party she canvassed for. Realising that she could fit in one, possibly even two babies and still just about reach the top of her profession by becoming a QC, she persuaded her newly wed husband, who had had a vasectomy eight years previously, to have a reversal (see page 103). This was successful and they had a son. Almost immediately after the birth Prudence, against the advice of her gynaecologist, decided to try for another and conceived a second child. Twelve months after the birth of the first baby, she had a daughter and had thus achieved, at the age of 42, the model boy-girl family, while still being on course for her 'silk'.

So far, so good. But her little son had never seen all that much of his mother, who had had to fit in quite a lot of work at the bar between her two maternities, and is emotionally handicapped by slight autism. He has seen much more of his father who, now in his sixties, has fortunately been able to work a lot at home and has a close relationship with his son. 'You don't realise till the second time round what you've been missing,' says Kenneth, admitting that his own mother has been nonplussed by the rapid turn of events.

He certainly sees more of the children than his wife does. Prudence gets up most days at 4 o'clock to read her briefs, before leaving for court at 8 o'clock. Arriving home for a late supper, she falls into bed exhausted. Kenneth and a full-time (but not live-in) nanny do virtually all the child care between them, including changing four-year-old William's nappies, but he seems to feel no resentment of his role. Fully committed and deeply emotionally involved with his children, he realises the importance of giving them both, and especially William with his problems, an emotionally secure time. His occupation and the stage of his career mercifully allow him to do this.

5

Last-minute childbearing and 'afterthoughts'

Some men become older fathers simply because they and their wives have postponed childbearing – or decided against having children and then changed their minds. Most women have great difficulty conceiving, especially for the first time, after the age of about 40. Hardly any women have children when they are over 44 – only about 500 a year in Great Britain. Relatively few (about 7,000) have babies in the 40 to 44 age range. As this biological cut-off point becomes imminent, some women, even after deciding earlier that they would be perfectly happy and fulfilled without having children, are suddenly struck in their mid- to late-thirties with a 'now or never' pang and rush to persuade their partners to allow them to have a baby or two and hang the economic consequences. Others have been tied up in their careers, and suddenly realise that time is running out for them. Since in the majority of couples the man is a few years older, this usually takes him over the Rubicon of 40 by the time he becomes a father.

In fact, most older fathers are only in their forties when their children are born, although it's the much older ones who tend to attract most attention: in Britain, over 33,000 men aged 40 to 44 fathered children in 1991, and over 10,000 aged 45 to 49. Only some 7,000 men over 50 became fathers.

Over the last 25 years, an increasing number of women, helped by more efficient contraception, have chosen to postpone both getting married and having babies. In the 1970s and 1980s, inflation and the rising costs of property and mortgages made many couples feel that two incomes were needed to sustain a reasonable standard of living. Instead of getting married in their early twenties like their parents, having babies straight away and living in poverty and sordid accommodation for many years, young people were enjoying themselves, were better dressed, better housed, had better holidays and more amenities than their parents had ever dreamt of. Many lived together but did not marry. Women who would once have found fulfilment in the home and the role of wife and mother went in search of satisfying careers, a new identity and self-fulfilment. The result was a generation of DINKies – dual income, no kids.

For such couples, babies didn't just mean broken nights and fewer evenings out – they meant less money as the wife gave up work, sometimes for many years, with little prospect of getting back on the same rung of the career ladder she had reached before the kids came along. The result, in any case, has been the postponement of childbearing by many women until their late thirties, by which time most of their husbands are well into their forties. Many definitely do find it harder work and more exhausting, but on the other hand they are mostly better off than they would have been 15 years earlier and can afford more by way of child care. In Britain, maternity leave legislation giving women more job security has been a big factor in encouraging working mothers to have babies later and then return to work.

In the United States, a new quarterly magazine, *ParentAGE*, was launched in 1993 and aimed at 'the new parent over 35'. It addresses the special concerns of older parents – from finances to health, sexuality and career juggling. 'The response has been pretty amazing since we started in May,' says editor Anne Adams Lang.

DECISIONS ON PARENTHOOD

Because of the possibility that his wife may assume that they will have children together, or even that she will suddenly want to have a baby just before it's too late, it is essential for an older man marrying a younger woman to make his attitude to the possibility of having children absolutely clear, and discuss plans as early as possible in the relationship.

Most couples agree about decisions on parenthood and 70 per cent of American couples even agree on the number of children they want. Those who disagree may be in for a rocky relationship, according to relationship counsellors: the best advice is to sort things out *before* a definitive decision to live together is taken, but this is not always done. Older men are particularly at risk of coming unstuck over this: they often have children from an earlier marriage and may have mentally closed the door on further family responsibilities; some will have had a vasectomy.

US research based on the National Survey of Families and Households suggested that 3.6 per cent of men want children although their wives want none, and 1.8 per cent of women want children but their husbands want none. But in couples where the man is older and already has children from an earlier marriage, the proportions are likely to be reversed – and more polarised.

'This is the number one issue for our organisation,' says Beliza Ann Furman, founder of the North American support network WOOM (Wives of Older Men). 'It's an awesomely emotional issue that can cause a tremendous risk for the marriage. The fact that your husband grew up on Sinatra and you grew up on Elton John is easier to resolve than whether or not to have a baby. When you're in your early twenties you may think you don't want to have kids, but in your late thirties you may change your mind. That would be about the time the older husband might be thinking of retiring. The last thing he'd want to worry about at that point in his life is how to pay for the education of an offspring.

'The average age difference between our members is 19 years. If the husband refuses to have children, that means these women are going to spend a considerable amount of their lives without a husband and without children.' About half of WOOM members who disagree on the issue finally do have children; of the remainder, many get divorced.

Ms Furman herself got married at the age of 23 to a 38-year-old dentist who had two daughters from an earlier marriage. At the time, she was a professional ice-skater and was unconcerned about having children. By the time she was 30, she had changed her mind. One day, after seeing a neighbour's baby in the park, she sat down and wept and decided to take things into her own hands. With 'premeditated forgetfulness' she conceived two days later. After the initial shock and a period of misery at losing his freedom and his 'lead spot' in his wife's life, her 45-year-old husband came round to the idea and became a devoted father of the couple's two children.

Like Mr Furman, middle-aged men sometimes underestimate the rewards to be had from late fatherhood, the

potential importance of children in strengthening a relationship, and their own ability to cope with the demands of
small children. They dismiss, or misread, the sometimes
coded signals from their partners, often expressing desper-
ation and a biological urgency that may be strong enough to
break the relationship if frustrated.

Jonathan, 60, has two children by his first marriage who
are now aged 31 and 33. When he remarried at the age of
46, his wife wanted to have a child but he didn't. For five
years he resisted: they had a comfortable lifestyle, with con-
tinental holidays and frequent evenings out at restaurants
or the theatre, and he rightly felt that all this would be
threatened by the arrival of a baby. He still remembered
with distaste his years of changing nappies and pushing
prams.

But his wife persisted and eventually a baby was born
after six years of marriage. As soon as the child arrived,
Jonathan was delighted. 'I never saw the others born – it
was an extraordinary experience.' His initial reaction was
that he felt rather inadequate and couldn't cope emotionally. He seemed to get tired more easily. 'But at another
level, I coped better. I sat up all night with him in my arms
when he was ill – I was calm when my wife was hysterical
with worry.' The child had a more privileged life than his
first children because he was better established and there
was more money available.

But tragically, his earlier resistance to the idea of having
a child seemed to have sown the seeds of destruction in their
relationship. His wife left him when his son was three and
they haven't lived together since. He sees a lot of his son,
now eight, and they go cycling together. 'He's delightful, I
adore him. But I find the separation very disturbing.' His
son is aware of his father's age and often talks about it, and,

like many other children of broken marriages, wonders why his parents don't live together.

If men who marry younger women are reluctant to have children with them, their partners may well feel cheated sooner or later. As one frustrated younger wife put it: 'He is always saying that sex with a younger woman is more exciting and how lucky he is; but he doesn't accept that having a baby or two is part of that.'

Sarah's husband had three children from his first marriage and convinced her to remain childless because he was absolutely adamant that he didn't want to 'go through all that again', but this is a decision she now regrets. 'I think we should have talked it over more and that I should have put my case more strongly,' she says. 'When I married him he made it plain that having children wasn't on the cards. I didn't mind at the time, but I think I do regret it now. He is likely to die well ahead of me and I suppose I can look forward to a lonely old age.'

Janet, now 40, married her husband when she was 35 and he was 48; he too had three children from his first marriage. 'It took his wife so long to agree to the divorce and we had so little money that I didn't really consider having children till it was almost too late. We did talk about it then but I think we were enjoying our time together and I could see that having a child would change everything. We didn't really make a concrete decision, it was just that time drifted by and now I think we're both too old, it would be unfair on the child. By the time the child was grown up I'd be 60 and Geoff would be 73; I think that's too old.'

It seems important for older men in new relationships not to be selfish in these matters, but to discuss intentions fully and not make assumptions or let things drift.

Occasionally the situation is the other way round with

the husband wanting children more than his younger wife. This was the problem faced by Pat, who married a man 19 years older than herself when she was in her twenties. Although her husband had three children from his first marriage, he was keen that they should have just one together. Pat saw herself as a career woman and was very ambivalent about having children. 'To be honest, I'm not sure that the fact that I thought he wouldn't mind not having children wasn't one of the factors I unconsciously weighed up in wanting to marry him.'

Pat thinks part of the problem was the 'generation gap'. 'He was happy with me, but I wanted more independence than the traditional kind of wife he had been used to, and this was part of the rift between us.' As often happens, a difference of opinion over something as fundamental as the desire to have a child or not to have a child tore the marriage apart.

AFTERTHOUGHTS

Some children are born not just to an older father, but to two older parents: they may be 'afterthoughts' or 'accidents' to a mother who thinks she is 'past it', or even come by surprise after all hope of having a child has been given up.

Kristin's parents were 45 and 44 when she was born. Her mother had been in a car accident and had been told she could never have a baby. She went from doctor to doctor who all told her the same thing. The thirty-first doctor she consulted said she could get pregnant and agreed to treat her.

Kristin, a journalist in her forties, says her parents were

overprotective. They had been teenagers in the 1920s, she in the 1960s. Her father in particular could not make the adjustment – he thought that whatever she did ('which was not *that* terrible!' says Kristin) was shaming for him. As a result, she had a very tense relationship with them. After she grew up, they became close again. Kristin got married late to a divorced older man who had had a vasectomy and has never had children herself.

Some people marry late because of wars. Sheila's parents married after the Second World War at 47 and 41: it was the first marriage for both of them. Her father had been wounded in the First World War, then went to sea until his ship was sunk early in the war in 1939. He then became a postman. With her older brother, she had a warm and affectionate 1950s' childhood.

'I don't think I gave any thought to my parents' ages during my early childhood . . . I accepted them as they were. But one day while rummaging around upstairs, my brother and I were astounded to come across our parents' marriage certificate and discover their ages. We must have been nine or ten at the time, which would have made Dad about 59 and Mum 53. I'd always thought of the girl next door, who was eight years older than me, as grown up. To be 59 or 53 was a concept we couldn't readily grasp. It was as if we had unearthed a secret.'

Sheila says that her mother, who came from a large family and had helped bring up brothers and sisters and nephews, was used to babies and small children. 'But it must have come as a shock to Dad to be presented with two babies in later life. They were both delighted to have us – but I'm sure she had more confidence.' Her father sometimes had a difficult time coping and relating to the children.

'When we were at college or starting work and beginning to spread our wings (or trying to!) – those were the times when I used to wish my parents were younger. I seemed to spend years telling them where I was going and what time I'd be back. My life seemed to revolve round the last bus. Everything was theirs as opposed to mine, and they couldn't bear me even changing things around in the house.'

Her parents grew old together, but it was while Sheila was in her twenties. As so often in the past – and to a considerable degree still today – it fell to her as a daughter to see her parents were all right and put them before her own life. This is surely worse if they are both older parents than if just the father is elderly.

'If both your parents are elderly, you get to know old age long before your time. I used to have a fantasy that on the day of my seventieth birthday I would revert to the age of 25 and live those ten years of my lost youth again. I've never had a baby. My child was 74, 75, 76, 77 and beyond . . .'

Later fatherhood seems to be a positive experience for men even when it occurs by mistake. One man who became an older father by accident at the age of 43 and dreaded the arrival of another baby explains how it happened and how his attitude towards his late offspring was transformed into one of appreciation and delight.

'Emma was conceived one spring morning at about 3.27 a.m.,' writes William, a university administrator married to an academic. 'I remember the time more clearly than the date: it was the first time I had had a sustained erection, the nervous tensions of lust and a responding mate, in more than a year of stress and sleeping pill addiction which had left our marital intimacy apparently a matter of historical regret and our comradeship perilously close to the rock of indifference.

'We neither of us contemplated conception. Our other children had been born over ten years previously. They had become good companions and were approaching maturity in their own styles, and would clearly flap free from the nest at the earliest possible moment. We were almost looking forward to it.

'When, a short while later, the unimagined proved imminent (abortion having been seriously considered and ruthlessly, proudly, rejected), the news created consternation. Our 13-year-old son dissolved in tears at the thought of domestic tranquillity being disturbed. I wept inwardly for sleepless nights to come, the deadly exchanges of fatigue-bred ill-temper, the limitations on leisure, and the painfully rediscovered routines. Spaces made in cars and hallways for prams and carry-cots, the smell of stale nappies, the hideous assault on middle-aged eardrums. I explored the depths of selfishness.'

He consoled himself with the thought that his new son – he always thought of 'it' as a boy – would make him lose weight and recover lost skills with footballs, cricket bats, sandcastles. He would enjoy reading Arthur Ransome again.

'It was of course a girl: fantastically ugly. And from the plain came forth love. The nappies and broken nights weren't that bad and were soon over. She grew quickly, hated football, spurned cricket, sandcastles and bedside reading. She was into ponies, a solitary vice, by the time she was four. We especially enjoyed the primary school period, making new friends and pretending to be younger than we were.

'Now, 18 years later, she is a woman, self-contained, independent of everything except my bank account, wilful, adorable. I hope she's happy. I am proud to have been her progenitor, to be her father. I must not reveal sentiment: she has a powerful vocabulary of street-bred vituperation and disdain. She plans to read physical anthropology; she wants to discover for herself how nature could have been so unfair as to give superwoman a wimp for a father.'

Other fathers can be surprised by success after years of trying. One unusual case reported in the *Observer* in 1993 was that of Sheila Dietrich and her husband, who had been trying in vain to have a baby for over 20 years. Exactly nine months after their silver wedding, when Sheila was 46 and her husband 52, their son Wayne was born. She didn't even realise she was expecting him until she was seven months' pregnant because she had put on so little weight. 'It was too late then to worry about whether there might be anything wrong with him. We just had to keep our fingers crossed.'

His parents don't think Wayne has missed out on anything because they're older. They've been able to spend more time with him. 'I like the way he keeps us in touch with what's going on in the world,' said his mother, now 63. 'He brings his friends home and they talk about music and bikes and books and I think it keeps us young.'

Wayne, at 16, speaks fondly of the security his older parents give him. 'Younger parents have got their lives much less sorted out. Half of my friends' parents have split up or are in the process of doing so, which leaves them either in one-parent families or having to deal with new step-parents. They find it very traumatic and unsettling. But my Mum and Dad have a rock-solid marriage and they own their house, so I feel safe.'

Another surprise birth was Joe, born in 1992 to Monica Boothman, then 44. She and her husband Bob had two other children, Louise, 22, and Sam, 21. 'I was incredibly surprised when I discovered I was pregnant,' she told the

Observer in 1993. 'We hadn't bothered with contraception for years, and when I missed my period I thought it was the start of the menopause . . . My son thought it was hugely funny and ran off to tell all his friends.

'Once I got used to the idea, I became very keen to have the baby. I would only have considered an abortion if there was anything at all wrong. I thought we were too old to cope with any kind of handicap, and if anything should happen to us, it would have been up to his brother and sister to manage, which wouldn't be fair.'

Bob, the older father, is 'besotted'. He had flatly refused to attend the birth of the first two 20 years ago, 'but with Joe he was there all the way through and he thought it was wonderful, which I'm sure has made a lot of difference to his attitude to the baby.'

When both parents are older, it seems very common for them to be perceived as old fashioned, out-of-touch and overprotective. One afterthought baby, Pippa, born when her eldest brother was in the sixth form, was embarrassed that her parents were 'older and more frumpy'. For a time she lived with a school friend and was surprised to see that her parents were always kissing and cuddling. 'I never saw much evidence of that in the way my parents were with each other. I think that was definitely because they were older and more tired.' There was 'no way' she could talk to her parents about contraception and sex. 'By the time I came along my parents had retreated from life in a way. It was all very quiet, sitting around watching the telly and cutting the grass.'

An advantage was that when she was adolescent the age difference allowed for a bit more indulgence and tolerance, 'because in some sense I wasn't as threatening as another woman in the family'. But when her parents became ill, she resented 'getting into caring much earlier in my life than most people – it's more natural for my brother, who's 50.'

One of the problems being the only child of older parents – noted by Kristin (see page 62) – is that 'you become the most precious thing in their lives, which is fine when you're young, but becomes harder later on when you leave home and realise that you'll never be as important in anyone else's eyes.' Even if they have older siblings, afterthought babies are often effectively only children, brought up alone by parents to whom they are particularly precious. Therefore an only child, arriving like a miracle just before the menopause when virtually all hope had been given up, often has a particularly hard time in adjusting to the effects of the hothouse relationship with his parents.

Crispin, a 46-year-old film editor who was born when his mother was 43 after 14 years of trying, remembers that he always felt different and even a bit embarrassed about his parents at school open days 'because they seemed old fashioned and fuddy-duddy'. He found his parents overprotective and claustrophobic. 'I'd taken so long to arrive that their biggest fear was that they might lose me.'

He has never been able to cope with failure very well and puts that down to having over-indulgent parents – 'It stamps on your ability to deal with adversity. Now, as a parent myself, I realise that one of the most important things you can teach your child is that life isn't fair and you don't automatically get what you want.'

Crispin recognises that his older parents were more secure financially and therefore able to do more for him than if they'd been younger, and that they had more maturity than younger parents. But his arrival must have put a strain on their marriage: 'They'd settled into a comfortable pattern, and when I came along after 16 years it was quite disruptive. I know from my own experience as an older father that change gets more difficult as you get older.'

Like other people who grew up in the 1960s, even with younger parents, he became aware as he grew up that his parents belonged to a 'totally different generation and were incapable of understanding where my interests lay'. Like many only children, he thinks his relationship with his parents would have been less difficult if he had had brothers or sisters, and doesn't think it surprising that he has followed in the same pattern as his mother by having a child in his forties. Now he finds himself torn between his sick mother and his 18-month-old daughter. 'I visit her most weekends but I still feel guilty. If I don't go my mother misses out and if I do my daughter misses out. My daughter will also miss out by not having that special relationship with a grandparent.'

The grandparent problem is one that especially affects children of two older parents: when only the father is older, there is usually one set of active grandparents present to provide children with the experience of that relationship.

6

The children of older fathers

The experience of older fatherhood is often much more positive for the fathers than for their offspring. That at least would appear to be the case for yesterday's older fathers – although perhaps those of today may turn out to be different.

Very little sociological research has been done into the effects of older parenthood on offspring. Virtually the only large-scale study ever made concluded that sons born to older fathers enjoy significantly higher levels of educational and occupational achievement than sons born to younger fathers. Published in 1989, this research analysed data from a US Occupational Changes in a Generation survey covering 25,000 American men. It concluded that because parents' education, employment and economic wealth improve with age, and because younger parents 'experience stronger competing role demands than older parents', parental age influences children's environment, and as a result, sons born to older fathers generally do better.

Another US study carried out in 1987, which looked at what it means to be the child of older parents, found that half the adults interviewed expressed either satisfaction about having older parents or felt unaffected by it; the rest felt their parents' age affected their lives significantly and, usually, negatively. On the positive side, they considered their parents more secure, emotionally and financially, than younger parents, and they mentioned that the quantity of time that parents or step-parents spent with their children was important to their sense of well-being. Negative perceptions included shame over older parents' appearance, the inability of older fathers to join in active sports, lack of communication (the 'generation gap') and concerns over parents' mortality. Few said they would choose late parenting for themselves or recommend it to others.

Certainly, many people today in their thirties, forties and fifties who were brought up by older fathers complain that their fathers were remote, authoritarian figures, forbidding, often bad-tempered, sometimes ill. Often they mention the bad effects that their fathers' inadequacies have had on their emotional and sexual development. On the whole, these fathers were not men who remarried after divorce or widowhood, but men who had simply married late, perhaps because of the war, perhaps out of loneliness, perhaps out of some feeling of duty that they had to continue their line. Those men who had really wanted children but had never married or whose first wives had been infertile were of course different, and most had close and warm relationships with their children. But even the ones who had previously had children and had remarried after widowhood or divorce often proved to have shortcomings too, perhaps because they didn't really want more children – but in those days, with less effective contraception, children often arrived anyway.

'Fathers were something other people had,' says Ada, now aged 48. 'I thought everyone's father was old and ill. I was surprised to hear of other children being taken on holiday with their parents, and doing things with them.' Ada's father was 58 when she was born and there were five children altogether, the last born when he was 65. He had been married before and was a widower. Ada's mother was younger than her father's eldest daughter and borrowed her wedding dress to get married in.

Despite his earlier family experience he didn't have a good relationship with his second wife and doesn't seem to have appreciated his children: 'We didn't bounce home ready to tell Dad all our news – we just had to keep quiet and out of Dad's way. It was not easy to have a meaningful father-daughter relationship in such circumstances.' Ada admits that much of his inadequacy as a father arose from his being ill rather than being old, 'but old people do get ill!'

Ada also married an older man (perhaps in a vain attempt to sort out 'unfinished business' with her father) but it ended in divorce. Looking for financial security as a single parent, she studied law, qualified as a solicitor and is now happily married to another solicitor the same age as herself. 'Everyone is advantaged and disadvantaged, and we all have to make the best of life as we can. I felt disadvantaged by having an older father, but others find it difficult to come to terms with their conventional upbringing!'

Ada's elder sister, Sheila, has much the same story to tell: 'I was scared of him, didn't know him as a person, and felt he lived in a different world from me. My parents both told me they hadn't wanted children and I got the strong impression that we were a burden. He seemed remote, but had to be obeyed. Threats of being beaten with his wide leather belt and terrible noisy rows between my mother and father were enough to frighten me into keeping quiet and out of the way.

'I felt alone and unwanted, and lacked both a true father figure (he was more like a grandfather) and any model of a normal husband figure. Both my brothers were much younger and as I went to an all-girls school, I had no experience of the role usually played by a man in a family. I assumed I would never marry — when I did it was to a younger man I saw basically as a friend. After my divorce I seem to have followed my mother's 'pattern' in that my significant relationships have been with considerably older men (still searching for a father figure?).'

The sisters recognise that there was a positive side: 'I think I gained a lot from those early introductions to older people in other walks of life, and especially being able to go abroad and stay with people my father had met on earlier travels, hitch-hiking round Europe before his second marriage,' said Ada.

Christopher, 39, was born when his father, a museum curator, was 47. He had married late and his younger wife complained that he often said he hadn't wanted children. 'He had a terrible temper and my mother always implied that he might get a heart attack, so we were always told not to provoke him. In fact, as we found out later, there was nothing wrong with his heart.' Having such a difficult, cantankerous father clearly did not foster healthy emotional development. Christopher married, but his twin brother is a confirmed bachelor and his older sister has never achieved a successful relationship with a man.

David, a radio producer in his fifties, was the only son of a diamond merchant who married for the first time in his forties. Although his father is now dead, he had such an intense dislike of him that he still cannot bring himself to talk about him. He was not physically violent, but evil-tempered and cold to David and his mother. David surmises that his mother was the only woman who would agree to marry him, and then only because she was 40 and desperate to have a child.

Mervyn Jones is the son of the distinguished psycho-analyst Ernest Jones, who was over 40 when he became a father for the first time. Although on the face of it, 'he was excellently equipped for learning to be a father', he found it difficult to adjust and proved to be not much good at it. His son comments with some exasperation: 'If he was so damn good at everything else, why couldn't he be equally good at being a father?'

AWARENESS OF AGE

Most children do not think about their parents' ages when they are small: they accept things as they are. But as they get older, and especially when they reach their teens, they often become increasingly aware of their older father's 'difference'.

Tom's father was 20 years older than his mother and he was born when his mother was 20 and his father 40. 'When I was a small child I didn't realise there was anything unusual about their situation and I wasn't at all aware of my father's age,' he recalls. 'But when I hit my teens I became aware that his attitudes were very different from those of the fathers of a lot of my friends. He was much stricter and wasn't prepared to listen to my arguments or let me wear strange clothes and muck around like my friends did.'

Robert's father, too, was 20 years older than his mother. 'I suppose that it was when I was about ten that I first realised my father was much older than my mother. Before then it didn't matter; he was just Daddy. I think it was only when I was in my teens and he became ill that it mattered, when he couldn't play football with me or do other things that fathers usually did. Because of his ill-health I used to worry that he would die before I grew up; in the event he died when I was 18 so I just made it. It wasn't the loss of him that was so bad as what it did to my mother; I don't think I saw her smile for nearly two years.'

Margaret, an only child who is now 38 with two children of her own, was born when her father was 43. 'But he was actually the son of a Victorian family, because he was born of older parents, 11 years after the next youngest child. Added to that, he spent much of his youth in the war – he was among the first to be called up and the last to be demobbed.' As a result, his life was ruled by feelings of duty, frugality and loyalty, and he was completely unable to relate to a teenage daughter in the 1960s. He had never learned to drive, never went on holiday and always lived in the same suburban house. He was overprotective and out of touch, and Margaret was motivated in her early adult life by rebelliousness and a desire to shock her staid older father. His parents had died before she was born, so she had only one set of grandparents. But her own children miss out too, because now her mother is too busy looking after her ailing father ever to come and see them.

Writing about his own family and his experience of older fatherhood, the art critic Tim Hilton makes the point that men changed by the experience of war were 'ever afterwards remote from their wives and children' – and this may well apply to men who only married after the war. 'Those of us who grew up in the 1960s', concludes Hilton, 'may have learned – unwittingly or not – to be flexible and helpful parents. This is one of the advantages of peace.'

Eva, too, had a father whose destiny was moulded by

war. A 45-year-old theatrical designer, Eva is the elder
daughter of Polish parents who came to London after the
war. Her father was 52 when she was born. He had been
imprisoned by the Russians in the 1920s and had lost his
hair after suffering frostbite escaping from a prison camp,
'so he was not only old, but completely bald, which made
him look even older!' When the Communists took over in
Poland, his business was confiscated and he and his young
wife left for London.

Eva recalls: 'He was an appalling parent. He related to a
different culture and a different generation. He could only
think of his need for male heirs (although he had nothing to
pass on any more). Once he said to us: 'I'd rather have ten
boys than you two girls!' He was half-joking, but it shocked
us.

'He found any kind of intimacy difficult to cope with,
and his sexual relationship with my mother seems to have
been disastrous. Once he sort of collapsed on the floor when
I hugged him and this made me conscious of his frailty. I
felt I never got to know him, although he didn't die until I
was 19. I was the favourite and I recognise, curiously, that
many actions in my life have been motivated by wanting to
please him.'

Eva has never married, although she has been successful
in her career and has cycled round the world. She feels that
her sister has been badly affected by her father's inadequacies: she has no self-confidence and is afflicted with a degree
of low self-esteem which effectively prevents her from leading a happy life.

Many older fathers of the past are often described as
strict and protective. Several of Charlie Chaplin's children
by Oona O'Neill have commented on how strict the great
man was as an older father. 'He hated the sight of a Coca-

Cola bottle and we weren't allowed to drink it,' remembers Annie, now 34. This could have been more to do with his hatred of the United States after he was banned from the country than with not wanting to spoil his children. But Annie adds: 'He wasn't crazy about babies. He thought children should be seen and not heard.' Annie was 11 when her favourite sister Josephine, then married and living in Geneva, had a baby son called Charlie. Annie was thrilled. Her father was pleased that Charlie was named after him, but 'Whenever Charlie screamed my father would say "Get that child out of here!" ' Annie would enjoy going to stay in Geneva to escape from her 'strict father', drink Coca-Cola and stay up late.

LOVED OLDER FATHERS

Many older fathers have extremely good relationships with their children and are remembered with affection and fierce loyalty, even when they die before the children are grown up.

Jennifer Grant, the only and much-wanted daughter of Cary Grant, was born when he was 62 and was a 20-year-old student at Stanford University when he died. Although Grant's marriage to Jennifer's mother, Dyan Cannon, ended when Jennifer was only three, she had a close relationship with her father despite a bitter custody battle. Grant had always wanted a family, but it was not until his fourth marriage that he succeeded in having a child, and he then felt cheated by the breakdown of that marriage. He worshipped Jennifer and once said: 'She's the best production I ever made.'

Now 28 and just married herself, Jennifer says that

hardly a day goes by when she doesn't think about her famous father. 'He's always in my mind, especially on great events in my life,' she says. 'When I graduated from Stanford I kept wishing he could be present. In the end I chose to *feel* him there. And it was like that on my wedding day – I was definitely in touch with him.'

The children of less glamorous older fathers often feel similar love and affection. Frank Taylor, born in 1906, was a brilliant mechanical and electrical engineer – he had six university degrees – and was also a sportsman and business brain. He was honoured for his work with young people and for helping to develop incubation units for premature babies. His first wife was unable to have children. When she died young, he remarried at the age of 57. His wife was 26 and he was one year older than his father-in-law. He and his wife had a son and two daughters: he was 59 when his son George was born and 69 when Victoria, his youngest, was born.

He was an excellent parent and saw a lot of his children since he ran his own business and worked mainly at home. His elder daughter Amelia speaks warmly of him: 'He was an amazing man – we idolised him. He was devoted to us – in fact he spoilt us rotten.'

He had always wanted to have children and was clearly delighted when he had them. Already successful in his business and personal life, he told friends: 'Now I'm fulfilled, now I've got everything.'

Although in his seventies, he was an active father, taking the children swimming every Sunday after church. But sadly the frailty of old age overtook him and he never lived to see his children grown up. His youngest daughter Victoria was three when he had a hip operation, five when he became ill with cancer of the larynx, and only eight when he died. But even after his tracheotomy, he would still read Victoria's bedtime story, putting his finger in the hole to help him speak, and would bring her her cocoa and her cut-up apple. Victoria 'went to pieces' for several years after his death.

While admitting to feeling the 'stigma' of an older parent when they were young, the girls miss him now that they're grown up. George, the eldest, now an engineer like his father, was 17 when he died and 'felt robbed in a way' that he didn't know his father as an adult. He still feels his influence, pushing him to achieve, but regrets that he is no longer there to assess those achievements.

Like many older fathers, he was felt to be overstrict and out of touch by his adolescent children – George remembers arguments about smoking and drinking. And yet in many ways 'Mum was the strict one – he always found something positive to say, even in a bad school report.'

Now, they wonder what he would have been like had he lived to see them grown up. Would he have been overprotective? Would he have approved of their choices in adult life? Would Amelia have felt she should have become a nurse rather than going into Lloyd's if her father had still been alive to influence her? Would he approve of her playing rugger like he did? Their father had a very strong presence – in some ways one which is felt from beyond the grave. 'He always used to say "I'll see you walk down the aisle",' says Amelia, 'and we believe he will be there.'

Was death worse than divorce? In some ways not, the sisters think. Victoria's friend Annabel was the daughter of an 'ideal' young couple, but now her father has left her mother and Annabel can't bear him.

Janice, from Ocean City, New Jersey, USA, was also the daughter of a widower who was 63 when she was born during the Depression. Her father was the 'active force' in her childhood. He taught her to roller-skate and bought her an extravagant bicycle during the war, teaching her to ride by 'dashing up and down the street steadying my seat until the wobbles were gone'.

She remembers relatives 'cluck-clucking over how sad it was that Ed would never see his daughter grow up'. But when she was a teenager, her dad was present at every dance recital, band performance and athletic event she took part in. He instilled in her a passion for learning and watched with pride her graduation from high school and college. At the age of 85, he was father of the bride and 'celebrated the birth of his grandson by arriving at the hospital with a baseball and bat to welcome the new arrival', eventually dying at the age of 97. Janice cherishes the 'rich legacy' of her older father.

Joe Wright, now in his twenties, is the son of the internationally known puppeteer John Wright, who founded the Little Angel Marionette Theatre in Islington, London. Joe's father was 65 when he was born and had already led a full life. Born in 1906 in South Africa into a strict Methodist family, John had started life as a chicken farmer. In the Depression of the 1930s, he and his partner had lost everything and he gave up farming and went to art school in Cape Town. By the time he met Joe's mother he had already been married twice, first in a marriage of convenience to a Jewish actress to enable her to escape from Nazi Germany, and second to a South African actress. This second marriage ended when she went back to work in South Africa and he stayed in London.

By the time he married Joe's mother, puppets and marionettes had become his life, and together they founded and built up the Little Angel Theatre in a bomb-damaged former temperance hall which they bought with a workshop and cottage for £700 in 1959. John had not had children before and apparently was so involved in his work that he almost had to be bullied into having any. But Joe says: 'He was an excellent father, with a lot more patience than most younger men.'

Joe was 'not really into football – perhaps because my father was in his seventies when I was at the football age. But I spent a lot of time with him in his workshop, making things.' As his sister was six years older, he often had to play on his own, almost an only child. But although his father worked extremely hard, putting in a 12-hour day right up until a year before he died, he was always accessible and Joe saw a lot of him when he was small.

As a man of artistic temperament who had rebelled against his strict upbringing, John Wright was an easy-going father and not overprotective towards his children. Perhaps because he continued working to the last, he lived in the present – although when he had his older friends round, Joe liked listening to him talking about his Bohemian life in Soho after the war when he was a scene painter at the Ballet Rambert and used to flirt with Margot Fonteyn and drink with Dylan Thomas. Like many older fathers, John Wright had developed his full potential late in life and was a stable, rounded personality by the time his children were born – a vastly different person, no doubt, from the young chicken farmer in the South Africa of the late 1930s.

Unlike some children, who feel the stigma of having a father old enough to be their grandfather, Joe was never ashamed of having a father who was so much older than most of his friends' fathers. 'I was quite proud of it and was never teased at school.' Having a father so much older has helped Joe come to the understanding that there are more similarities than differences between the generations. 'I spend a lot of time trying to piece together my father's life – after all, when I got to know him he was already in his late sixties. It's given me a very long perspective, thinking back to his youth which was apparently so remote from the world of the 1990s. I think one's perception of what it is to be a man is coloured by what your father is or does or was.'

Joe and his sister never had any grandparents. 'My father's parents were dead long before I was born and my mother's parents were in South Africa and I only saw them once. But because of my parents' lifestyle, which revolved entirely around the puppet theatre, we had a sort of extended family of the friends of the theatre which made up for the lack of grandparents.'

Joe does regret that his father died before he had properly grown up and, like many children of older fathers, remembers fearing his father's illness or death when he was a boy, thinking of his father as something precious and fragile. 'When I was eight or nine, he fell through the glass roof of the workshop and hurt himself quite badly. I was always afraid of something terrible happening to him.' (See Afterword.)

7

Sex, fertility and vasectomy reversal

OLDER MEN AND SEX

Many older fathers – or fathers-to-be – and especially men who have married younger women, worry about their sexual performance, particularly as they get older. Worries about sexual performance can also be linked to fears about fertility because of the common confusion in people's minds between virility and fertility. Of course, fertility is linked to sexual performance in men since it depends on the ejaculation of semen. But a greater worry normally to the older husband is whether they will be able to satisfy their younger wives in 15 or 20 years' time. Will they, in their sixties, still be up to it when she is in her forties, supposedly the sexual response peak time in women? Are they likely to become impotent? Will their wives need to take a lover? Will they still be potent and fertile if a last-minute baby is wanted?

Men who worry about their sexual performance are usually thinking in terms of their physical response which inevitably alters with age. It is generally true that an older man takes longer to achieve an erection – perhaps minutes rather than seconds. The erection may not always be so hard as that of a young man. There is some reduction in the volume of seminal fluid: in men over 50 the amount ejaculated will vary more than it does in younger men and will usually be less, only measuring 1 to 3 millilitres instead of the young man's 3 to 5 millilitres. Ejaculation may be delayed.

Orgasm may feel different for the older man: the sensation a few seconds before ejaculation that orgasm is inevitable may not be so marked. The forcefulness of ejaculation is also reduced and there may be fewer contractions of the penile muscles. Older men may lose their erection more rapidly and there is also a longer period before another erection is possible – while a young man may be able to achieve another erection within minutes, in an older man it may be a matter of hours. None of this is likely to make any difference to a well-adjusted couple.

There is much erroneous information about sexuality in older men. One American book on 'mid-life sexuality' said that men over 60 did not experience erection of the nipples and men over 50 did not experience contractions of the anal sphincter muscles at orgasm, and that men in their fifties and sixties are unable to have erections within 12 or 24 hours of ejaculation. For many, perhaps most middle-aged men who have an active sex life, these statements are patently untrue.

A West German book on male sexual problems confidently asserted that 'fewer than ten per cent of men over 60 have normal sexual potency (defined as having normal sexual intercourse without difficulty at least once a month)'. This has been clearly contradicted by many studies of sexuality. More realistic estimates of impotence range from 20 per cent at 60 to 80 to 85 per cent at the age of 85. But impotence at any age has much more to do with psychology or lack of a suitable partner than with physiology. Although ageing does have some effect on erection, sex therapists Masters and Johnson claim that the male 'does not lose his facility for erection at any time'. Sex for the older man does not have to become any less pleasurable for himself or for his partner – and often the reverse is true.

In a healthy man, active sex can continue into old age. There is evidence that the more sexually active a man is, the less likely he is to lose his potency. According to Masters and Johnson, impotence in older men is mainly caused by 'sexual boredom and fear of failure'. In many marriages it is the woman who loses interest in sex and the man feels unable or unwilling to insist. Society's attitude that sex between older people is somehow not nice doesn't help older people achieve a satisfying sex life into old age. Sex may even help to prolong life: a study of the elderly carried out by Duke University in North Carolina, USA, found that frequency of intercourse was a significant predictor of longevity for men. Another possibly related finding is that men who remarry after the age of 60 tend to live longer than men who don't.

While it is true that a lot of older men retire from sexual activity or develop sexual problems, this is sometimes because the wife does not want sex. This may be because she has hang-ups about sex, because she does not love her partner or the relationship has deteriorated into boredom and lack of desire, or because she feels that sex is inappropriate for someone of her age. After the menopause many women suffer from vaginal dryness, and intercourse, if attempted, may be painful. Perhaps not realising that a vaginal lubricant (such as KY Jelly or oestrogen creams) can usually put matters right, the woman is put off and no longer encourages sexual advances. Disappointed, the man gives up and a vicious circle is set up. This is why marriage to a younger woman may act as a tonic for a middle-aged or older man's sex life.

POTENTIAL SEXUAL PROBLEMS

Men, like women, may develop sexual problems because of fears about the decline in their sexual powers with age. It is easy for a cycle of failure to be set up after just one or two unsuccessful episodes. Perhaps they attempt love-making when the man is tired, has drunk too much or is worried about a situation at work. The man cannot get an erection or loses his erection before he has completed sexual intercourse. He is worried by this, and this sets up a pattern of stress and fear of failure that makes him fail a second time round as well.

Most women can help a man out of this cycle if they accept the situation and don't put pressure on him to get an erection and have full sexual intercourse. The most successful technique used to cure psychological impotence is known as sensate focus. The couple are told they must not attempt intercourse, but stroke and caress one another, first of all without touching the genitals and then more intimately. With the stress of worrying about performance removed, most men find they are easily aroused. Some find that the fact that intercourse has been forbidden makes it more exciting for them and they resume full intercourse faster than the therapist has 'allowed'.

Another problem for some older men who are trying to have a baby is retarded ejaculation or even failure to ejaculate altogether, despite having no problem in achieving and sustaining an erection. The problem usually has the same cause: the man's concern with his performance. Older men usually take longer to reach orgasm, and the man who is anxious about this may find that as orgasm approaches he becomes so concerned that he loses pleasure in the sex act and therefore fails to ejaculate. If his partner is upset and concerned about this, another vicious circle of failure can be set up. Again, the solution is to enjoy sex, to set aside time for it, and to concentrate on pleasure and not performance.

Some older fathers feel anxious about sex because of the way other people react to them. Older fathers have shown the world they are still sexually active and a lot of people feel disturbed by this. There is the stereotype of the 'dirty old man', a feeling that there is something wrong and out of place in an older man who is interested in sex, especially in sex with a younger woman or which results in a baby.

But while healthy older men – even old men – should have no problem with sex, the risks of illness clearly increase with age and this can affect a man's sex life. Coronary heart disease is one of the most common causes of death and ill-health in Western men. Men aged between 45 to 64 are three times more likely to suffer from heart disease than women. A heart attack can be a devastating event for any man and often affects his sexuality for a number of reasons, mostly psychological. Recent studies show that 60 to 75 per cent of couples decrease or stop sexual activity altogether after the man has suffered a heart attack.

Most of the reasons for stopping sex are to do with fear – fear that exertion during sex will lead to another heart attack. After a wait of 16 weeks or so, most men are told they can resume sexual intercourse. During averagely active sex the heart beat ranges from 90 to 160 beats a minute – the same as light to moderate activity and should therefore present no problems. Couples are often told to use sexual positions in which the man does not exert himself so much.

Many doctors, however, fail to realise the full effect of fear on the sex lives of couples where the man has had a heart attack. Often inadequate counselling is given. Sometimes remarks made by a doctor can make things worse. One doctor told his patient recovering from a heart attack that it was very unlikely that he would have a heart attack during sexual intercourse, but that if he did he could comfort himself that it was a great way to go! This thoughtless remark came back to him time and time again when he wanted to make love to his wife and obviously created problems for them both.

There are some illnesses which lead to physically based impotence. Diabetes is one, although usually the disease has to be quite severe or long-lasting before problems occur. Other causes of physical impotence are radical surgery, trauma or pelvic injuries, hormonal problems and multiple sclerosis. Alcoholism can also result in impaired sexual performance and impotence.

In many cases it is the drugs used to treat these conditions that can cause problems; it is always worth discussing this with your doctor to make sure that where possible the drugs chosen do not affect sexuality and that you are given as low a dose as possible. Drugs which may cause impotence or failure to ejaculate include some diuretics (often used in the treatment of heart disease), beta-blockers and other drugs used in the treatment of high blood pressure and angina, opiates (used for pain relief), sex hormones used to treat hormonal disorders and prostate cancer, monoamine oxidase inhibitors used to treat depression, and ganglion blocking and neuro-muscular blocking drugs used in the treatment of Parkinson's disease.

Men who suffer from impotence for physical reasons may

still be able to enjoy sex. Just because a couple cannot have full sexual intercourse, they can still cuddle, caress one another and use other ways of stimulating one another. A man can still feel very pleasurable sensations without getting an erection and he can still give pleasure to and satisfy his partner. It is also possible for many older men to have an orgasm without having an erection.

For those who feel that vaginal penetration is vital to their sexual fulfilment, physically based impotence can be treated with penile implants and with drugs. An increasingly used treatment is the injection of papaverine (a derivative of opium) into the spongy part of the penis, which causes a long-lasting erection. Once the correct dose for the individual has been established, men can be taught to give themselves the injection before they want to make love.

THE POSITIVE SIDE

Setting aside the problems, however, many men find the sexual side of their relationships more fulfilling as time goes by, and many women agree with this.

'Having been married to both a man my own age and then to an older man, all I can say is that sex was far better second time around,' said one younger wife. 'I think an older man is less concerned with his own pleasure and more concerned with yours – or rather, he takes pleasure in giving you pleasure.'

Many men who marry younger wives say that their sex lives are much better and that they are having sex as frequently, or more so, as they did when they were younger. Not only may older men have fewer sexual hang-ups and prove to be more considerate lovers, their slowed sexual response, which means that they take longer to reach orgasm, is an advantage for many women, especially if they can achieve multiple orgasm. Premature ejaculation, which is common in young men and a frequent cause of frustration and sexual disharmony in younger couples, hardly ever occurs in men over 50.

One thing that seems certain is that the longer a man has satisfying sexual relations, the more virile he will remain. One US academic work, *Handbook of the Psychology of Aging*, maintains that 'amounts of past sexual activity and enjoyment are excellent predictors of sexual activity and enjoyment in old age.'

FERTILITY WORRIES

Prospective older fathers, even those who already have children, may worry that their fertility is not what it was and that they may have problems having children with their new younger wives.

Fertility is not normally a problem for men in their fifties or even sixties. As men age their sperm count does gradually decrease, but it is usually high enough to impregnate well into their seventies, and men have been known to father children into their nineties. Lower sperm motility may sometimes be a problem in older men: good motility is as important for fertility as the sperm count itself. Decreases in the male hormone testosterone take place very gradually – if at all – with age and there are wide variations from man to man. Men who have had a prostatectomy may be infertile, and men who have had a vasectomy should realise that this operation is not always successfully reversible: both these conditions are dealt with below.

A recent record may have been set by Les Colley, who was pictured in the magazine *Marie-Claire* in 1992 holding his eight-week-old son Oswald. At that time Les was 92 and his wife Patti was 38. Les's other son, Norman, from his first marriage, is in his seventies.

Les said, 'I could live for another 20 years and I'm sure I will. The doctor says that I'm in better shape than a man of 60. I'm a teenager at heart.' Patti, his wife, added, 'I wasn't surprised that Les could father a child. He's quite a good lover, actually, better than some younger men I've had. I think Les will live for about another 10 or 15 years, but it would be a pity for the baby not to see his father as he grows up.'

Unlike women, for whom the risk of giving birth to a handicapped child increases markedly in their late thirties and forties, older men seem not to run the risk of having a handicapped child. However, there is some evidence that there are a few congenital conditions which are linked to having an older father. One is a rare form of dwarfism called achondroplasia. There is also some evidence that Down's Syndrome is slightly more common in children conceived when the man is over 55.

Infertility in men is probably as common as infertility in women, although much less attention is given to it as it is usually less treatable. For every 100 couples who are infertile – infertility being defined as when a couple have regular intercourse without conceiving for over a year – in about 50 cases it will be the woman who is responsible, in 40 cases the man and in 10 cases both. The most difficult form of male fertility to treat is a low or absent sperm count, which is usually unexplained. Some men produce large numbers of abnormal sperm, which lowers their fertility. Others produce sperm which seem normal but which swim poorly or seem to have difficulty in fertilising the egg.

Infertility is very distressing for a man whatever his age because society tends to equate virility with fertility, and men have a hard time admitting that they may have a problem. The older man may be even more sensitive about this than younger men, partly because he sometimes comes from a generation when sex was not discussed as freely as it is now, and partly because he may have fears anyway about his virility or about how other people see him. While in most infertile marriages, people tend to assume that it is the wife's problem, people may not think the same if the man is in his fifties or sixties.

The discovery that a man is infertile can be devastating for him as well as for his partner. In an older man it can be particularly destructive because it can affect his whole self-image. Robert was 43 when he married for the first time. Before this he had had a long-standing relationship with a woman who didn't want children and this had been part of the reason why the couple eventually separated.

Robert's wife Sara was in her thirties and very keen to have a child. After a year in which nothing happened, they were referred by their GP for infertility tests. Robert's semen sample showed that he had a very low sperm count. 'We asked what were the chances of Sara conceiving and were told that the chances were greater of my being run over by a bus.'

Robert says that his whole view of himself changed overnight. 'Because Jane, my previous girlfriend, never wanted a baby, we were always scrupulous about using contraception. All those years of pills, condoms, panics and rushing out to get pregnancy tests because Jane was a few days late now seemed pathetically unnecessary. For a whole month after Sara and I got the news I just couldn't bear to make love. Sara was very sympathetic and understanding, but every time we tried nothing happened. I just didn't feel like a man any more. I was terribly depressed.'

Like many men who have a low sperm count, Robert and his wife opted for artificial insemination by donor, or donor insemination, known as DI. DI is not a cure for infertility, but it is a way of bypassing it, enabling the couple to experience pregnancy, birth and bringing up a child, although the father knows the child is not biologically his. For some men this is a problem; for others it is not. Most children are not told that their biological father is an unknown donor and there is a lot of secrecy surrounding it, which can create problems as the child grows up.

'At first, when Sara got pregnant, I did have fantasies about the father of this child and I suppose I did have some feelings of jealousy. But when the baby was born all that faded away. Henry is now two, there's no question that I'm his father, that he loves me, that I am bonded to him. I can experience all the joys of being a father, Sara is so happy and fulfilled, and what does it matter about my genes? We're planning to do the same thing again for a second child. We've only told a few close friends and family, and I no longer get pitying looks from people. The most extraordinary thing is people are always saying how much Henry looks like me.'

Helen opted for DI because her husband had had a vasectomy after his two children were born to his first wife. An attempt to reverse it failed and Andrew, aged 51, agreed that Helen at 33 should have the opportunity to become a mother before it was too late. Helen says, 'Everything has been fine. Andrew accepted Samuel from the start. After all, he accepts that I have to get on with his daughters and that we're not a conventional family. He says that anyway Sam feels just like his son, he's not aware of any difference and that he'd love Sam anyway because he's mine. I don't know if I will ever tell Sam. After all, by the time he's grown up Andrew will be 70 or may not even be here any more and there wouldn't seem to be much point in upsetting things. As far as I'm concerned Andrew is his dad and that's all there is to it.'

Infertility in men is usually not age-related, but like many other conditions it can get worse with age. A man whose sperm count was low but adequate when he was in his twenties may find that by his late forties or fifties his fertility has dropped too low to make pregnancy likely. A worrying development is that sperm counts have been falling throughout the developed world, possibly due to exposure to oestrogens in the environment − in food and in the water supply − and this must inevitably reduce the leeway that older men have benefited from in the past, because normal sperm counts in younger men have in the past been many times higher than those needed to achieve pregnancy.

Most low sperm counts are very resistant to treatment. Various kinds of hormone treatments have been tried, but with a very low success rate. Some studies even showed that the treatments reduced the man's chance of conceiving. Many of the drugs have unpleasant side effects such as loss of libido, swollen breast tissue or loss of body hair, so that most men do not persist with treatment.

One technique which has been used with some success to help infertility when the man has a low sperm count is the 'split ejaculate' technique. The first part of the man's semen which is ejaculated is richest in sperm. If the first parts of several ejaculates are pooled together, and then introduced into the woman's vagina through artificial insemination, the chances of pregnancy may be increased. The 'test tube baby' technique or IVF (in vitro fertilisation) and a variation of this procedure known as GIFT (gamete intra-fallopian transfer) both offer a greater chance of fertilisation for a man with a low sperm count because the sperm can be mixed with the egg rather than making the long and difficult journey through the woman's reproductive system. Micro-insemination, where sperm is placed inside the outer walls of an egg which is then transferred to the uterus, is another method recently developed, but the pregnancy rate so far is low – between 5 and 25 per cent.

Male infertility can also be a result of a sexually transmitted disease which was not diagnosed and treated early enough, from undescended testes, again undiagnosed, and very occasionally as the result of a complication of mumps. Secondary infertility – infertility which has developed in a previously fertile man who has fathered a child – can result in later life from other causes. Secondary infertility can be caused by a falling sperm count, by sexually transmitted infections such as gonorrhoea, or a varicocele – a kind of varicose vein in the scrotum.

Varicocele is probably the most common cause of male infertility: 14 per cent of all men have varicoceles which increasingly impede sperm formation and transport. Among men with fertility problems who have never fathered a child (primary infertility), 35 per cent have varicoceles; among those with secondary infertility (men who have fathered at least one child but can't reproduce again) as many as 80 per cent will have varicoceles.

Repair surgery is possible but experts disagree about the results. Dr Marc Goldstein of the Cornell Medical Center in New York says that 80 per cent will have improved sperm counts and improved sperm motility. 'In my experience, 43 per cent of the wives with no infertility problems of their own will become pregnant within two years of their husbands' procedures,' he says. But other US experts claim that surgery makes little difference.

If the cause of infertility, secondary or otherwise, is blocked tubes, perhaps caused by infections, it is possible in some cases for these to be repaired by microsurgery.

PROSTATE PROBLEMS

One of the commonest complaints for middle-aged and older men – and which causes a great deal of anxiety about sexuality and fertility – is enlargement of the prostate gland. In all men over the age of 45 the prostate does enlarge to a greater or lesser extent, but in some men the gland enlarges in such a way that it presses on the urethra, the tube which carries urine from the bladder through the penis, restricting the flow of urine. If untreated, this obstruction can cause bladder infections and stones, and sometimes eventually kidney damage. Early symptoms are those of bladder stress – the need to get up, sometimes several times, to pass water at night, frequent urination during the day, impaired stream, small volume of urine passed; and occasionally the need to urinate suddenly or urgently.

Until quite recently, the only available treatment has been surgery – one reason why men tend to put up with their symptoms rather than seeking medical help. But now, although surgery will remain the treatment for most men for some years to come, drugs are now on the market which can improve symptoms in some but not all cases. Outpatient hyperthermia (heat treatment), which shrinks the gland and relieves symptoms, is also suitable for some men.

There are a lot of misconceptions about prostate problems and one that should be nailed straight away is that the prostate operation is likely to cause impotence or other sexual problems. However, one likely side effect of the operation is functional *infertility* because the ability to ejaculate semen in the normal way may be impaired or lost.

The modern prostate operation, known as transurethral resection of the prostate, or TURP, involves a four- or five-day stay in hospital. During the operation an electric arc cutting device with fibre optic vision is introduced through the penis and the obstructing part of the prostate (not the entire gland) is cut away. It is a straightforward and safe operation which is usually successful in removing the obstruction and resolving the bladder problems. Most men are told to have a month off work and not to take part in strenuous activity – including sexual intercourse – for this period of time.

Infertility is a common result of the operation because semen is ejaculated harmlessly back into the bladder at orgasm instead of outwards in the usual way. But orgasm itself is not affected, and the man's enjoyment of sex is almost always unimpaired.

If a prostate operation threatens and fertility is an issue, the couple should discuss the possibility of alternative treatments. Two types of pill can now be prescribed by GPs: alpha-blockers (usually one called indoramin) which reduce the pressure on the bladder sphincter and improve urine outflow; and Proscar which slowly reduces the size of the prostate by reversing the process which causes enlargement. These drugs – and the hyperthermia treatment – do not work, or work sufficiently, in all cases. But they will usually afford some improvement in symptoms which will take you off the 'immediate surgery' list, and although the improvement may only be temporary it will usually last long enough for you to achieve a pregnancy.

Alternatively, sperm can be banked before treatment although this service is unfortunately not usually available on the National Health Service. There are also (expensive) medical techniques which can retrieve the retro-ejaculated sperm from the urine for artificial insemination, so having another child is not absolutely ruled out.

Prostate problems can also cause difficulties in a relationship. One younger wife recalls: 'At first he concealed it from me. I think because it was an 'old man's disease', although he was only in his early fifties. The problem was, I wanted another child. When we were told he should have the operation they didn't even bother to tell us that he might become infertile. When he asked about sex, the consultant just said, 'Oh, it won't affect your sexuality.' I only found out about the fertility problem through reading about it in a book in the library. The doctor was very taken aback when we said we wanted more children; he didn't know what to suggest.'

VASECTOMY REVERSAL

Vasectomy is a very popular method of contraception, with 90,000 to 100,000 operations being performed in Great Britain every year. However, it is simpler to do a vasectomy than to undo it, as many would-be older fathers have found to their cost.

Over the last 20 years many more men have 'taken the snip', perhaps because it is a less complicated procedure than female sterilisation (tubectomy), perhaps because men are now prepared to take more responsibility for family planning. The number of vasectomies increased in Britain during the mid- to late-1970s after a new law in 1972 empowered local authorities to provide the operation for social reasons on the National Health Service. Despite the advantages of male sterilisation, in 1970 seven women were sterilised for every three men. By 1976, the ratio had narrowed to seven women to six men, and by 1989 the figures were roughly equal. Most men who have it done are in their thirties and forties, and have decided that their families are complete. However, a relationship that seems perfectly satisfactory and stable when the operation is done may have deteriorated five or ten years later, perhaps when the children become adolescent or the wife's post-childrearing career really takes off.

More often than not, divorced men form relationships with younger, pre-menopausal women, perhaps 10 or 15 years younger, or perhaps only a few years younger. Many of these women will want to have a child with their new partner, often even if they already have children. Apart from the strong urge to experience birth and having children which many women experience, a younger woman may also feel that joint children – much more than any stepchildren which either partner may bring to the marriage – will help to cement the relationship and provide her with a family to focus on during her (statistically probable) long widowhood.

The older man has a strong responsibility to sort out the matter of childbearing before he gets too deeply involved with a younger woman. Does he *really* not want any more children at any price? If so, he must say so clearly and not fudge things. If he feels that, despite reluctance, he could probably be persuaded, all is likely to be well: most men in that situation seem to come round to their wives' views and become willing, often enthusiastic, fathers second time round.

If he has had a vasectomy and his potential wife is keen (or thinks she might become keen) on having babies, the matter is more serious. Vasectomies cannot always be reversed and even when the procedure is physically possible, the failure rate is around 50 per cent or higher.

When 22-year-old Pam Clift met 46-year-old company director Roy, who was a father of two and had had a vasectomy, she didn't worry at first because she 'wasn't thinking in terms of a permanent relationship and the vasectomy was very convenient'. But as things grew more serious and they started living together she 'started to get a little broody . . . I'd always wanted children and I'd always assumed that I would get married and have a family.' Interviewed in the *Sunday Mirror*, Pam admitted, 'As our relationship developed and we discussed having a family, it was becoming a problem . . . For a couple of years, Roy said he was not ready to have a reversal. He was very reluctant. When he had the vasectomy, he'd made the decision that he had completed his family.

'At one stage, I thought we would never have children and for a period of about six months I was very depressed . . . I never got to the stage of feeling resentful, but I would have done, I'm sure . . . if we hadn't agreed on children, it would definitely have caused problems.'

Roy had been upset at 'losing' his children when his first marriage had broken down and didn't want to risk going through all that again. 'It never occurred to me I would have the operation reversed or even that I'd ever have another child.' He had made the decision once and for all and had understood that it was irreversible. But he slowly realised that having the vasectomy reversed was something he had to consider as his relationship with Pam developed.

It was obviously a difficult decision for Roy. In the *Sunday Mirror* interview he even evinced a certain squeamishness in explaining his reluctance. 'There are always risks in any operation and having an anaesthetic. It wasn't a major consideration, but I did think about it.' He went so far as to say that he didn't think the relationship would have suffered if he hadn't decided to go ahead. In the end, of course, once the thing had worked he was over the moon. 'It's wonderful starting another family, and our relationship with my two other children has improved enormously since.'

THE PROCEDURE

Before contraceptive sterilisation is carried out, the doctor or surgeon should always make clear that the operation should be considered a permanent one. Vasectomy is a very simple and straightforward procedure, and perhaps for this reason some men may imagine that it is just as quick and simple to reverse. Reversal is not simple: it is expensive (and unlikely to be available on the National Health Service) and does not always succeed. It is estimated that around 5 per cent of vasectomised men later regret their decision, so the number seeking reversal seems likely to rise in coming years.

Success in reversing vasectomy depends first of all on how the operation was originally done. Until fairly recently, it was quite usual for surgeons and GPs to remove a section of the vas (the tube that transports the sperm from the testicles) and tie back both ends of the remaining tube. This provided the virtual certainty of contraceptive success, because after a section is removed it is impossible for the vas to 'recanalise' itself and cause an accidental pregnancy. But it also makes the reversal procedure difficult or impossible.

Once requests for reversal reached sizeable numbers – they have been rising steadily and currently stand at around 1,000 men a year in the UK – the operation began to be done in ways that are more easily reversible using clips or diathermy (heat sealing). In fact, the most usual method nowadays is diathermy which has been common for over ten years. Reversal surgeons are helped by this because nothing is 'missing'.

The reversal – called vasovasostomy in medical language – is usually carried out under general anaesthetic with an overnight stay in hospital, although some surgeons do it under local anaesthetic, with sedation if the man is anxious. It is a fiddly procedure, usually done by microsurgery, and takes approximately two hours. Joining tubes are inserted to reconnect the severed vas canals on each side and the joints are sewn up with silk thread. 'It is a dry operation', says Mr Naveed Hasan, who does three or four reversals every week under local anaesthetic at the Surgical Advisory Service in Harley Street, an organisation that has been doing reversals for ten years. 'There's little blood – we try to preserve the fine artery that runs above the vas to improve healing. We normally do both sides – that improves the chances of getting a useful sperm count.'

The cost of the procedure (which is rarely available on the National Health Service, although it does occasionally happen that budget-holding GPs will authorise payment in exceptional cases, according to Mr Hasan) is £1,200 at SAS. The British Pregnancy Advisory Service charges £945 at their nursing home in Brighton, inclusive of one night's stay and preliminary tests.

Even when the recanalisation is completed successfully –

which happens in 80 to 90 per cent of cases – sperm transport may be prevented by thickening of the wall in the vas. Another potential problem is the antibodies which are produced as a response to the sperm being absorbed into the bloodstream following vasectomy: this can result in sperm which is damaged or has low motility. Motility is actually more important than sperm numbers, says Mr Hasan: 'If you have only two million sperm but they have good motility, you can quite easily get your wife pregnant. High sperm counts are no good if under 20 per cent have good motility.'

Both fibrosis and antibodies are greater hazards the longer the time that has elapsed since the operation was done, and if it was done more than ten years earlier the chances of success are considerably reduced.

After the reversal operation, patients should take things easy physically (absolutely no sex) for three weeks, but then all should be back to normal. Semen tests are done after six weeks and 12 weeks and, if necessary, after six months. If sperm counts are too low, a course of steroid hormones may be given to stimulate sperm production and another test done in three or six months. After that, things are unlikely to improve and it's best to give up.

One procedure sometimes done when sperm counts are low or sperm motility poor is to take a semen sample by masturbation and have it 'washed' and treated; it is then used for insemination at the time of the wife's ovulation. Sperm can also be taken from the epididymis (the coiled tube above the testicle where the sperm mature and are capacitated) and are treated and used for insemination. In theory this can be done every two months, but it costs over £3,000 a time.

Kenneth, divorced in his early fifties, got married again a few years later to Prudence, a barrister aged 40. The couple never discussed the question of babies until after they married – in fact Kenneth never thought it was on the cards because he had had a vasectomy. Prudence had not been married before and had never have time to think about babies because of her work at the bar. But soon after their wedding she explained to Kenneth that vasectomies could be reversed and why didn't he have a try as she would like to have a baby?

Kenneth had never heard of reversal, but he was willing to look into it. He contacted a urologist he knew at the golf club who confirmed that it could be done (although not always successfully) and advised private treatment 'because you don't want to waste any time at your age'.

Two days in the Middlesex Hospital and Kenneth's plumbing was repaired. After a month or two, tests pronounced his sperm sparse but viable. At the second or third try at insemination with his 'washed' sperm, his 42-year-old wife, her fading fertility boosted with hormones, conceived and a baby was duly born by Caesarean section under epidural anaesthesia, with the delighted Kenneth looking on. He pronounced the experience 'unmissable', and within a few months they had achieved pregnancy number two. Soon they had the 'perfect family', a boy and a girl. Kenneth turned into resident house-father, getting up four times a night, and Prudence went back to her briefs. (see Chapter 4). Kenneth was lucky: most medical experts rate the chances of successful reversal at only 30 to 40 per cent, although Mr Hasan claims a 50 to 60 per cent success rate.

If vasectomy reversal fails, the only alternatives are donor insemination (see page 93) or adoption (see Chapter 8).

8

Stepfatherhood and adoption

STEPFAMILIES

Some men become stepfathers when they remarry and find themselves as 'older fathers' to children not biologically their own. Step-relationships can be notoriously difficult at the best of times, but for older men the situation is often complicated by the fact they have children of their own by an earlier marriage and/or by the arrival of the children they have with their new partners. They may be, all at the same time, fathers-first-time-round of children they are now separated from, stepfathers of their second wives' children, and older fathers of children by their second wives.

The usual arrangement on divorce is for children to stay with their mother, and when a divorced father remarries a woman who has children of her own he may suffer the double trauma of being separated from his own children and being resented by stepchildren for whom he is expected to act as a father. As one stepfather put it: 'I didn't just marry the mother, I married the children too.'

Like the stepmothers of fairy-tales who wreak havoc on the lives of their stepchildren, stepfathers also have a bad reputation to overcome. The image of a stepfather in many people's minds is cold, uncaring or even brutal. It is not helped by the fact that stepfathers are frequently the offenders in the child abuse cases which from time to time hit the headlines, such as those of Maria Colwell and Jasmine Beckford recently in Britain. Research shows that stepfathers are more often involved in child sexual abuse than natural fathers and are more likely to be violent towards their stepchildren. All this can create considerable anxiety in men who are becoming stepfathers on marriage.

Unlike stepmothers, whose stepchildren are usually in the care of the natural mother most of the time, stepfathers are more likely to find themselves taking on a paternal role. Since the natural mother is most likely to have custody of her children, her partner is also responsible for their day-to-day care. Relate, formerly the National Marriage Guidance Council, estimates that at least a third of fathers have lost all contact with their children following a divorce, and this means that many stepfathers are to all intents and purposes performing the role of father, replacing the natural father completely. In other cases, the presence of a real, sometimes actively involved and occasionally bitter and destructive father can create many problems for a stepfather.

Where the stepfather is largely responsible for his stepchildren, he will have to play the role of father in many ways. He has to face a difficult double-bind; if he acts in a paternal role, he can be accused of trying to replace the natural father, and if he doesn't, he can be accused of being ineffectual or of washing his hands of the stepchildren. Stepfathers are far more often expected to discipline their stepchildren than stepmothers, and this creates a particular dilemma for many stepfathers; whether to act and be seen as interfering or unkind, or to stand by and leave discipline to the mother and be seen as passive, uninvolved and uncaring.

Discipline is one of the biggest areas of contention in most families and in stepfamilies this problem is exaggerated. In the typical nuclear family, fathers tend to think mothers are too soft with the children and mothers think the father is too strict and authoritarian. However, in most families the mother, being there most of the time, tends to handle discipline, only turning to the father when things get out of hand. The father is then given the task of laying down the law.

A father who can't put his foot down with the children is usually resented by the mother. But with a stepfather things are difficult. He may feel he can't be too hard on the children because they are not 'his'. He may be afraid that if he is hard on them they will resent it and think he doesn't care for them. The mother has to be both mother and father to them in a way and this is very stressful. The stepfather then feels he has no real role.

'Forging a relationship as a stepfather is very difficult,' recalls Henry, now 51, who became a stepfather at the age of 45 to two children from his wife's first marriage who were seven and nine at the time. 'I met them only after their parents' divorce was announced to them and despite attempts to take things slowly we were fairly quickly plunged into a new ménage together. It was okay when everything was nice, like when we all went swimming or went out on an outing together, but the problem was trying to create the ground rules at home and try to get them to do what we wanted. I can't tell you how many times they flung "You're not my father" at me. The first time it hurt but by the end I just said, "I know that, but you still have to do as I ask sometimes." '

When the stepfather is older than the natural father, as is frequently the case, this just provides an extra negative comparison, sometimes an extra insult. When the natural father is absent, the stepchildren may have quite unrealistic expectations of their stepfather. Heather felt her second husband, Simon, faced real problems at first when he married her and became an instant 'father' to her two girls. 'They hardly ever saw their father, so when I remarried they were both really keen to have a proper father. But they saw him really as a kind of fantasy figure. It took a long time for them to realise that he was really a human being who wasn't perfect and didn't always get things right.'

Comparisons between the natural father and the stepfather are always made and can cause difficulties. 'They're always saying things like, "Dad would never do that," or "Dad would be able to mend it," and things like that,' says one stepfather. 'It does tend to drive you a bit mad.' There is little the poor stepfather can do about this except be patient and hope that things will improve in time, which they often do.

Another problem encountered by many stepfathers is the need always to keep something in reserve, never actually to lose your temper or say what you think. 'Rachel is very sensitive,' says John, aged 55, whose stepdaughter is seven. 'I've found that even saying something as simple as "I think you've watched enough television for one evening – can't you go and do something else?" can be treading in a minefield. Sometimes when she is being really awful – especially when she is shouting at her mother – I just want to say, "Oh, shut up, you revolting child", and I would if she was mine – but I can't, in case she thinks I really do think she's revolting. There isn't that basic love and trust you have as a natural parent; you're always on trial.'

Stepchildren have already had to cope with one broken relationship and this can also lead to insecurity in the second, making stepfathering additionally stressful. 'Their father left them once, so they're always afraid, deep down, that I'll do the same,' says Derek, stepfather to two young boys. 'I am always having to reassure them that every row or bad day doesn't mean it's going to be the end of everything.'

These days remarriage is much more commonly the result of divorce than the death of a spouse. However, some fathers do become stepfathers because of the death of the the their wife's previous partner, and this can cause additional problems. Although the former partner isn't there to cause rows or dissent, enter into custody disputes or to resent the stepfather's involvement with his children, he is very much present in the children's minds and still exerts an influence.

When a father dies, it is very common for the children to idealise their dead parent. Their mother, too, may tend to idealise him, thinking of all his good points and not the bad. This can be very problematic for a new husband and stepfather, who may feel he is always being compared with this ideal figure and always falling short.

Marilyn's first husband, Derek, died at the tragically early age of 44 from cancer, leaving two children aged six and eight. Two years later she remarried Ray, a divorcee of 48. 'It's a bit like living with a ghost,' says Ray. 'From the beginning I think they were always comparing me with their dead father. We got on well, but somehow their dad always seemed to have played football better, let them stay up longer or watch more television. It was very hard always to remind myself that they were just kids, that they didn't mean to hurt me and that they couldn't behave any differently.'

Sometimes problems arise over inheritance. 'Derek had left a will, knowing he was dying, which left a lot of the family property to his wife for her lifetime and then to the children. I found this very awkward, because it meant that a lot of things weren't mine to use in case they got damaged, or dispose of if I didn't like them. There were certain things of Derek's that I couldn't touch. It was a bit like living in a museum.'

It's important to realise that a step-parent has no legal rights over his stepchildren, even if he lives with them and is responsible for their care on a day-to-day basis. This can lead to problems in certain situations; for example, a step-father may be unable to give consent to medical treatment if he is in charge of his stepchild at the time of an illness or accident, and he may be unable to sign permission for the child to take part in certain activities in school. A stepfather may have strong views on the child's education or other matters, but legally his views cannot be taken into account.

One option to get around this difficulty for the stepfather when the father is either dead or absent is step-parent adoption, which means that the stepfather becomes an adoptive father and bears full parental responsibilities for the children. At present it means that the biological parent, usually the mother, has to adopt the child formally too, although there are plans to make this unnecessary in future British legislation.

Legally, step-parent adoption is a comparatively straightforward process. But it is something which needs careful thought and consideration. Holly, who is Asian, had one child by her former husband who is black and then married Alan, who is white, when her first son was ten. The couple then had a baby together when she was 35 and he was 42. Her first son Rory saw very little of his father, but the fact that his father was black seemed to be very important to him and it was obvious to anyone that he could not be

Alan's biological child. Holly was aware of the importance for him to acknowledge his racial background and keep whatever links were possible with his natural father. Although Alan had a good relationship with his stepson, and Rory's natural father did not object to an adoption, the couple did have worries that his father might want to have closer links with him in the future and that a stepparent adoption might make this more difficult.

INTIMACY IN STEP-RELATIONSHIPS

Stepfathers may find they have an easier time with stepsons than with stepdaughters. With boys stepfathers may be able to provide some rough and tumble, interest in sports and male toys and hobbies, computer games, model railways and the like, which helps them forge a bond. Many stepfathers are conscious of the fact that there is a sexual element in their relationship with their stepdaughters, especially when they become teenagers. This element is present between natural fathers and their children as well, but is usually less difficult because of the bond which has been present since birth and the very strong incest taboo.

Occasionally the relationship between stepfather and stepdaughter can stray out of the father-daughter relationship and a sexual relationship can be established, either abusive or not. The case of Woody Allen and his grown-up stepdaughter Soon-Yi has publicised this possibility recently, and many women's magazines and newspapers have run articles by other couples to whom this happened. Normally such relationships occur between stepdaughters who were adolescent or older when they met their stepfathers.

Of course this situation rarely occurs, but quite frequently stepfathers can be uncomfortably aware of sexual feelings between them and their stepdaughters and that this can cause problems between them. Most stepfathers find that they cannot be as physically affectionate with their stepchildren as with their natural children. As one stepfather puts it: 'There's a kind of barrier. I haven't changed their nappies, I haven't given them a bottle, brought up their wind or sat with them in the middle of the night when they were ill . . . They've never snuggled into bed with us in the morning and they're too old now, they never will. It's even difficult to kiss them goodnight. It's a pity, but that's the way it is.'

Some stepfathers say that there is also a problem in expressing physical affection to their wife in the presence of stepchildren. 'I accept that it makes them uncomfortable and I have to respect that. It somehow seems wrong to them for their mother to be sexually active with a man who is not their father.'

Research shows that children with stepfathers tend to do less well in school, have lower aspirations and want to leave school earlier, and this especially applies to boys. This is not true of children with stepmothers, so cannot be entirely due to the effects of divorce per se.

Older fathers who become stepfathers may face particular problems because the children are likely to be older when they come on the scene – and most stepfathers seem to agree that the younger the children are when they first become involved with them the easier it is. Another factor may be that the larger generation gap makes it harder for the stepchild to accept the new relationship.

Becoming a stepfather to adolescents is particularly difficult. Most teenagers rebel against their parents but this is easier to do when the parents are in a stable situation to rebel against. If the parents' marriage breaks up, the child may have to cope with the adults' traumas just at a time when they want to work out their own. The appearance of a stepfather on the scene at this time can lead to stormy confrontations.

Most stepfathers of teenage children accept that the biggest mistake is to try to replace the natural father. 'I think you have to accept that, even if the kids never see their natural father, that you aren't and never will be their dad. You have to find yourself a different role,' says one older stepfather. 'With my stepchildren I can be a friend, an adviser, and of course I can sometimes tell them what they can and can't do – but there's always a distance. In the end my wife does do most of the laying down of the law because the kids won't accept it from me and it would simply spoil things if I tried.'

With younger children, especially if the natural father plays little role, the stepfather does stand a better chance of becoming accepted as a father figure. 'My stepdaughter was four when I came on the scene and she saw her natural father very seldom as he worked abroad. She seemed to accept me well from the beginning and now I don't think she can remember a time when I wasn't her dad. We have a child of our own now and I really can't say that there's any difference in the way I feel about them. We're just like any other family.'

The arrival of a natural child of the two new parents may create some problems for stepchildren, though sometimes it can create a bond too. 'When my wife gave birth to our son her two daughters were all over him, and it created a blood bond between us all because their brother was my son. The arrival of the baby seemed to bring the whole family together.'

The closer bond the father naturally feels for his new biological children doesn't necessarily create a problem with the stepchildren. One stepfather who has a stepson and a biological daughter from his current marriage observed: 'There's a stronger bond in my relationship with my daughter since it started at birth. So I feel more responsible for her problems. I personalise things with her and I am more objective with my stepson. But he doesn't resent this.'

In other cases the usual sibling jealousy can be magnified, especially if the stepchildren see their stepfather pouring affection on his natural child while showing restraint towards them. As for the relationship between stepchildren and biological children, that is best left to the children themselves to sort out. Any kind of pressure for them to 'like' each other because they are half-siblings is likely to be deeply resented and counter-productive.

Teenage stepchildren may be revolted at the arrival of a new baby, both because it confirms the fact that their parent and step-parent are sexually active and because the fuss over the new arrival seems out of proportion. Messy nappies and exhausted, preoccupied parents can seem the last straw when worrying about first boyfriends or girlfriends and crucial exam results. Many teenagers feel that they have invented sex, and the sight of older parents and step-parents procreating can create embarrassment. As one stepchild who was in her teens when her mother remarried said, 'I felt as if my mum and stepdad were producing their own grandchildren.'

Most stepfathers agreed that it takes time to be accepted. 'I think it takes at least two years to gain a child's confidence, and it's particularly difficult with teenagers because they're trying to rebel and become independent just at the stage that you are trying to get to know them and become a parent,' says one stepfather of a teenage girl.

Although family relationships can be complicated when there are two sets of children – his and hers – from two previous marriages, the greatest difficulties are probably faced by older stepfathers who have never been fathers in their own right. They have to adjust to being parents as well as step-parents. Many have quite unrealistic expectations of how children should behave and cannot cope with the sudden assault on their lifestyle caused by the presence of noisy, demanding children with apparently trivial interests and demands. They often don't realise that the rudeness, messiness and belligerence of their stepchildren is not something they should take personally and that the children would often behave like this with their natural father. But if the stepfather lets it get to him, and the children find they can make him insecure, these problems may escalate.

'I made the mistake of taking things too seriously,' says Brian, who became a stepfather at 45. 'Every time my stepson came out with something awful I would sit down and have a serious talk with him about how his mother and I loved one another, about how important it was to try and work at our relationship, and so on. It was a sure-fire way to get lots of attention. It took a long time before I realised what was going on and could say, like any normal father would, "Oh just shut up." '

So are there any rewards to being a stepfather? Despite all the problems, most stepfathers would say that in the long term there are. Most stepfathers and children in the end come to have an affectionate relationship, or at least to forge some kind of relationship of respect and companionship if nothing greater. For some stepfathers, the relationship seems no different to being a biological father, especially if they knew their stepchildren from a young age. Most people become parents not to pass on their genes or live through their children but to experience the trials and rewards of parenting and this is equally possible in a step-parent relationship.

'Things haven't been easy,' says one stepfather, 'but when I came back from a business trip recently and saw the expression of joy on my stepdaughter's face when I came in through the door I realised that it had all been worthwhile.'

ADOPTION

Although some couples prefer to face the difficulties of adoption rather than undergo invasive and uncertain fertility treatment, for most older men adoption is usually the last resort. Conventional adoption is almost always closed off to them. Most adoption agencies, whether local authority or private, set upper age limits for parents to adopt babies or young children, and often the upper limit is as low as 30 or 35. Some agencies may not allow divorced men to adopt, regardless of whether they have had children in a previous relationship or not.

The fact is that in Britain and North America today, with universal access to family planning and abortion, there are very few babies born who are recognised as 'unwanted'. In Britain in 1991, only 900 babies were adopted soon after birth, compared to 12,500 in 1968. Discounting step-parent and relative adoptions, the total number of children being adopted in Britain is now some 3,500 a year.

Local authorities make sure that the few babies available go to young families, not because older parents are necessarily thought of as less suitable, but because the adoption agencies have to restrict the numbers of couples applying and also have a duty to find the best possible family. Since adopted children have already lost one set of parents – their birth or natural parents – the agency wants to ensure that the possibility of losing a second set of parents is minimal.

In some cases, it may be possible for couples where the man is older to adopt older or 'problem' children. There are a large number of teenagers seeking adoptive families and children with handicaps or social problems may be placed with older parents. Otherwise, the only other option is adoption from abroad, with all its expense and uncertainty – and even that is currently very difficult because of local authority attitudes towards older parents.

However, a recent British Government White Paper, *Adoption: The Future*, published in November 1993, offers a crumb of comfort to older parents seeking to adopt. While stressing that authorities and agencies 'should satisfy themselves that adopters have a reasonable expectation of retaining health and vigour to care for a child until he or she is grown up', the text expresses concern that recent practice has been too restrictive, particularly in overseas adoptions. It emphasises that 'rigidity of approach is out of place. Parents in their forties may well have much to bring to the care and upbringing of adopted children.' The White Paper, which will form the basis for new adoption legislation, also promises to simplify the procedures for inter-country adoption and give local authorities a new duty to help parents seeking an overseas adoption.

A rigid age limit clearly causes problems for many couples – especially those who have tried to have children, undergone fertility tests and treatment and then turned to adoption. 'We married when Brian was 35 and I was 28. By the time we'd decided to have a child I was 30, by the time we realised we had a problem I was nearly 32, by the time we'd had tests and treatment which failed I was 34 and

Brian was 41. We were both considered too old to adopt.'
This is the catch-22 situation that many would-be adoptive
parents face today.

One lucky older father, James – possibly one of the last
men in his fifties to adopt from a local authority – describes
how he was able to adopt from a London borough in 1980.
'We fostered the baby from the age of two weeks, always
with a view to adopting. It's an agonising process because
you always know that they may refuse permission to adopt.
Of course, I was worried that they'd use my age as a reason
for refusing adoption – I was 53 at the time and my wife was
36. Fortunately all was well – in fact, they didn't seem very
concerned about my age – and we finally adopted Betty
when she was two. My wife was trained in child care, which
may have helped our case. But I know how lucky we were: it
would never be possible today.'

The authority even asked the couple to foster another
child with a view to adoption, but James had 'decided
against it – entirely because of my age. It's very strenuous
and I decided one was enough.' James had never had children and investigations after he and his wife had tried
unsuccessfully to conceive for a number of years revealed
that he had a low sperm count. 'I don't know what I would
have done if we had been unable to adopt Betty, because I
knew how vital it was to my wife and the marriage for us to
have a child: it was critical. I recognised it then and have
been reminded of it regularly ever since. We might have tried
to adopt from abroad, although that wasn't much done in
those days: I would have gone to whatever limits I could.'

How has the adoption worked out? 'She's been a source
of non-stop happiness, joy and satisfaction. I write her a
poem for her birthday every year.' James is sad that other
older fathers have so much difficulty adopting these days.

He thinks that being an older father 'is better all round. You've arrived, you're more yourself than a man in his twenties or thirties. You're likely to have more money, be less distracted by watching football, drinking in the pub, chasing the girls! You want to be at home more, so you see more of the children. If you're like me, you'll be more domesticated than when you were younger – more likely to share the cooking and household chores. That's got to be better for your child – and for your marriage.'

Roger, now 66, and Liz, 55, adopted two children from Latin America, Carlo, now ten, and Maria, seven. They had spent several years trying to have a family, but Liz had repeated miscarriages. 'If you know you're definitely infertile, you can probably come to terms with it,' said Roger. 'But with miscarriages, you feel there's always another chance. In the end we decided to try to adopt, but we were both to old to be considered for adoption of British children – I was 55 and Liz was 44.'

Through US connections, they were put in touch with an adoption network in a South American country. They then discovered with horror that a local law specified that adoptive fathers had to be under 50, but their lawyer dismissed this concern: 'You're not in the United States or Britain now: we'll take care of it.'

Before long, things were sorted and they came home with a three-month-old baby boy whom they soon adopted without problems. But when they took up the offer of another baby from the same source a few years later, things didn't go so easily: the local authority's attitudes towards transracial and international adoptions had changed and the adoption proceedings were delayed. 'It was very, very difficult. All kinds of obstacles were put in our way – they even threatened to make the child a ward of court. Maria was five before the adoption finally went through.'

These difficulties have more to do with the attitudes towards transracial and international adoption by social workers, local authorities and some adoption agencies than with the age of the father. But foreign babies are now virtually the only ones available for older fathers because of ageist prejudices against them, and now the barriers are up there too.

Things may be somewhat easier in the United States because many adoption agencies there, reacting to competition from private lawyers, have raised the previous cut-off age of 40. Each state has its own adoption laws, many offering few safeguards for the children. The National Council for Adoption is planning a major advocacy and public education effort in 1994 to get changes in the unsatisfactory laws prevailing. Private lawyers are the most hopeful way to approach adoption in the United States because the birth mother can choose with whom the baby is placed through them and more babies are offered through lawyers than through agencies. It's costly though: the mother receives medical and living expenses during the confinement which can run to US$15,000 and that's on top of the lawyer's fees.

It's also agonising, and the process can take a heavy emotional and financial toll. Traditional agency adoption involves two waiting periods: one for the agency to accept you (no guarantee, especially if you're over 40) and another for the agency to find you a child – which may never happen. Independent or private adoption certainly offers more hope to older parents, but couples should have no illusions that it's going to be easy.

'I've worked with families who have no concept that the adoption won't go ahead smoothly,' says Steven Kirsh, President of the American Academy of Adoption Attorneys.

'Once they've found a birth mother, they start buying clothes and decorating the nursery. But about half the birth mothers I meet change their minds.' And he advises: 'Don't believe you're going to have a baby until the moment you hold it in your arms.'

Gregg, 43, and Angie, 38, had to wait a year before they were able to adopt – and that's not a long time by adoption standards. 'There were a *lot* of ups and downs. It put a strain on our relationship,' Gregg admits. 'We'd argue, sometimes over frivolous things.' Angie agrees that the wait was awful, especially coming after failed infertility treatment. 'It took over most of our lives,' she says. 'That was all we talked about. I was very envious of everyone who had a baby. The envy and jealousy put me and Gregg at odds. He didn't understand it.'

Such experience is common. After they've been through infertility treatments, a couple will believe adoption has got to be easier. When they discover the risks and the financial stakes involved, it shakes them. They also feel out of control. 'Most people who adopt are older,' says Miriam Vieni, an adoption counsellor in New York State. 'They're bright. They are used to controlling their lives. Neither with infertility nor with adoption do you have control. For some, that's the hardest part.'

International adoption is still possible in the United States, although it is increasingly difficult and some agencies which used to specialise in this have recently all but given up because of the complications and the cost, putting it beyond the reach of most couples. Although attractive to older husbands because some countries have an upper age limit for adoptive fathers as high as 65, international adoption compounds waiting anxieties with worries that the baby offered may prove to be sick, or even that the country may change its policy on adoption. That has happened with a number of countries, most recently Romania and China, which provided American couples with hundreds of baby girls in the latter part of 1992 but clamped down in February 1993 pending a policy review. There is also the worry that local laws may be 'bent' by adoption lawyers, as with Roger and Liz (see page 119), or that a poor mother may be given money to induce her to part with a baby. Prospective parents may find it difficult and expensive to be sure that they are not involved in some racket run by an unscrupulous lawyer.

Money can of course talk when it comes to adoption, as with anything else. Many of Hollywood's rich and powerful have used their money and influence to arrange adoptions to replace the babies they have left it too late to have. The adoption agencies are wary of Hollywood adoptions, not least because of the high divorce rate. Bill Pierce, President of the National Council for Adoption in Washington DC, says: 'The difference between agency and private adoption through lawyers is simple. Our job as an adoption agency is to find families for children, not children for families . . . We believe that children have a right to the best family that can be chosen . . . Because someone is a Hollywood star or a wealthy person should not exclude them from the opportunity to have a family. By the same token, their wealth or their position should not exclude them from the same scrutiny any family undergoes before they are given a child.'

For most stars, however, private adoption is the obvious route and it is suspected that their money can help get their babies quicker. Said one adoption lawyer, 'It's nothing for a Hollywood star to come up with US$75,000 to jump the queue. Celebrity lawyers deny it, but it happens all the time.'

Certainly, it would seem unlikely that 67-year-old comedian Jerry Lewis and the ex-dancer he married after divorcing his wife of 36 years would have been able to adopt their baby girl through an agency. Age was not a problem either for billionaire media magnate John Kluge, 67, and his third wife Patricia when they adopted a baby boy in 1983. That marriage has since broken up and the child lives with his adoptive mother. Burt Reynolds was well over the usual adoption age when he and Loni Anderson adopted a son, Quinton, four years ago — now the subject of a tug-of-love case following an acrimonious divorce.

Unusually, 'LA Law' star Susan Rattan was actually present at the birth of her adopted son Jackson. She arranged to adopt privately when she heard through a relative of a baby who was going to be given up for adoption. She and her husband, Randy McDonald, are in their mid-40s.

But this kind of adoption — like all private adoptions except those between close relatives — has been illegal in Britain since 1982. It is now no longer possible for a couple to adopt a baby they know of through a friend, clergyman, doctor or relative, as was often done in the past: all adoptions have to be arranged through approved agencies or local authorities.

9

Financial and health problems of late fatherhood

Obviously, late parenthood brings its problems. For many older fathers, the most serious ones are the financial implications which are deep and long term. As one very old father puts it, 'Our worst problems are those which money could cure.' In an employment culture which puts a premium on youth and tends to discount the advantages of age and experience, redundancy and unemployment are real dangers for the older father. The risks of ill-health and of dying obviously rise as one ages. Other problems are more subjective and mainly relate to how well the man adapts and adjusts to his new situation.

FINANCE

The financial responsibilities of becoming a father later in life can be quite onerous. At a time when his contemporaries are seeing their children leaving home, their mortgages dwindling to insignificance and their wives embarking on successful second careers, the older father will often be saddled with substantial new housing loans, a wife spending most of her time looking after small children and only working part-time at best, heavy life and health insurance premiums, and often facing the prospect of forced early retirement or even redundancy with only a slender chance of finding alternative employment.

'It is something I worry most about,' says Edward, 56. 'I am supposed to retire at 65, but my employers have recently had one of those US business school-type clear-outs, with virtually everyone over 60 (except the chief executive, of course) forced to take early retirement and voluntary severance terms offered to many in their fifties. But I've got three children under ten and a massive mortgage which will only be partly paid off by the time I retire. Early retirement just isn't on the cards – in fact, I shall need to keep working till I'm 70 if my children are to go to university and we're to have a decent standard of living.'

A colleague of his, the same age with 20 years' service, has jumped at the chance of early retirement. With grown-up children and a small mortgage, he and his wife are going to India for a three-month holiday and he is looking forward to having the time to read and pursue his private interests. Edward says he can't even allow himself the luxury of feeling jealous: 'Having the children has brought its own rewards. I just have to live for them.'

Alan, 54, speaks of the 'narrowing range of options' in his life. 'Partly this is a function of age, because job possibilities for anyone over 50 are strictly limited. But there can be no question for me of giving up my rather boring, routine office job and going freelance, or doing voluntary service overseas. Perhaps it is a good thing: before I had these responsibilities my life was a mess!'

Premature death is a potential hazard everybody faces,

but older fathers have to think more about this eventuality since the probability rises with age. They also have to make proper provision for their dependents, which of course will be more expensive than if they were younger. It is useful to look at what may happen financially to women widowed by the early death of their older husbands.

Pensions

Janet was 24 when she married her husband who was 12 years older, and they had five children together. He died at the age of 57; she was 45, and all the children were still at school or university. 'To my horror I discovered that the civil service pension would not be paid to a woman under 50, although I did get an allowance for the children.'

Another widow, Margaret, found that her husband's pension scheme allowed them to pay the pension at a lower rate if a man's spouse was more than ten years younger than him. 'I suppose they argued that they would be paying it out for longer so they could give me less – and I do get less,' she says. 'Although the children were through their schooling, they still needed help with things; I'm sure my expenses are greater than they would have been if I had been the same age as my husband when he died.'

This provision is found in many 'final salary' or 'defined benefit' schemes, the type most commonly found in the public and private sectors in Britain: it does not apply in the 'defined contribution' or 'money purchase' schemes more common in the United States. Usually, the rules give the trustees of the pension fund the discretion to make an 'actuarial reduction' of the pension of a spouse more than ten years younger than the member. This means that the bigger the age gap, the bigger the potential reduction. But trustees may not always exercise this option and are unlikely to do so for as long as there are dependent children. Of course, even when children are no longer 'dependent', they may still need support in getting themselves established, as Margaret found. In a few schemes, the rules do not allow discretion, it is simply done. Other schemes do not have such a provision at all.

Again, some pension schemes will pay a widow's pension for life. But many will discontinue the pension if the widow remarries or even sets up house with someone. And a few will only pay it until she starts drawing the state pension at 60. A prudent older father will sort out these matters with his employers or the fund trustees to avoid the possibility of nasty shocks later on, and, if necessary, make extra provision through life insurance or an additional voluntary contributions (AVC) pension top-up.

Certainly an older husband, especially one with dependent children either born or intended, has a special responsibility to provide for his new family after his death, and the earlier he does so the cheaper it will be. Apart from sorting out his pension arrangements (may his ex-wife have any kind of claim on it?), the most important thing is the need for adequate life insurance because he must face the real possibility of his dying before all his children have completed their education.

There are all kinds of policies available to provide lump sums, family income for a specified period, regular sums for children (which may be available not just for school fees but to meet other expenses of a broadly educational nature), as well as annuities for the surviving spouse.

Extra pension contributions should be made where possible: in Britain, these are linked to the salary scheme in the case of full-time employees and known as AVCs (see above). One advantage is that they are highly tax-efficient: tax relief is given at the highest rate for contributions and a tax-free lump sum can be taken on retirement. And total allowable contributions range up to 40 per cent of gross salary for people over 60. Self-employed people, or even people in full-time employment who have a self-employed source of income, can have a separate private pension plan which is just as attractive from the tax point of view but has the added advantage that the pension can be deferred to any chosen age.

If a previous marriage has ended in divorce, it is preferable for the divorce settlement to be of the 'clean break' type, or an ex-wife might turn up years later with a claim on a life insurance pay-out, pension or even a family inheritance. A man who remarries must of course remake his will and he is allowed to do this beforehand 'in contemplation' of his remarriage.

It is also worth remembering that 'actuarial probabilities' are not certainties: older men can outlive their wives. Philippa married Brian, 12 years her senior, at the age of 38 and they had two boys. But she died of cancer at 51 with her sons still at school, and Brian had to take early retirement to look after them.

Younger wives should give special thought to the extra funds that would be needed should *they* die with dependent children who have to be brought up by their older husband, perhaps already on a pension and with no means of increasing his income. Fortunately, this kind of protection is relatively cheap for younger women, and if it is written in the form of an endowment maturing when the youngest child completes his or her education, it can provide a useful capital sum for her own retirement. And it is worth remembering that endowment policies can also be a cheap way of raising a loan, without actually cashing the policy in, if one is needed.

Unemployment

Redundancy, forced early retirement, invalidity and unemployment are other hazards for older fathers. Today, there are far fewer older men in employment both in Britain and the United States than there were in the past. Early this century, 70 per cent of men *over* 65 were in employment of some kind, as against around 15 per cent today. Since the 1960s there have been big declines (of over 40 per cent) in the proportions of men aged 60 to 64 in employment in both Britain and the United States to a current level of around 45 per cent, and smaller but still substantial reductions for men aged 55 to 59.

Of course, many of these unemployed older men have retired quite willingly, with 'enhanced' pensions. But the fact is that the contemporary employment 'culture' on both sides of the Atlantic effectively puts pressure on older men to 'make way' for their younger colleagues who are assumed, not always correctly, to be more vigorous and progressive. This culture also means that older men find it virtually impossible to find suitable employment if they do become unemployed. This is especially so in Britain (as distinct from the United States) because, although racial and sexual discrimination are against the law, it is not illegal to refuse to employ somebody on account of his or her age.

Matthew, 60, with an eight-year-old daughter, decided to take an early retirement package at 55 from his local government job to concentrate on his painting. It was fine at first, and he enjoyed the extra freedom, but five years later things don't look so rosy: his wife is beginning to resent being the main breadwinner and he wishes he had remained employed for longer.

Guardians and wills

All parents, but particularly older fathers, should nominate a guardian for his children in the case of both him and his spouse dying, as could happen in a road accident or plane crash. But it is important that both spouses agree on the choice and that their wills agree on this point. It might be a close friend or relative, but in any case make sure that the person knows about the arrangement and agrees to it and, that if he or she is married or has a partner, that person also knows and likes the children and is willing to support the relationship.

The will should also contain provision for a trust to be set up to support the children until they have completed their education. Make sure this is adequate: the guardian may need a bigger house, a bigger car or extra domestic help.

When, as is more likely, your younger spouse survives you, problems may still arise because at the time of your death some of your children may need greater financial assistance than others. Your eldest child's education may be complete; two other children may still be at school; one might need special tuition or medical treatment. The usual arrangement is to bequeath specified amounts only to off-spring who have completed their education and the rest to the surviving spouse to spend as she thinks appropriate. But you can protect this capital for your children – your wife might remarry, which could create problems – by setting up a trust or trusts to provide an income for their upbringing, with a distribution of the capital when they complete their education or when your wife dies. This may not be worth doing unless your estate is likely to be fairly substantial. Good legal advice on all these matters is essential.

But even when, as sometimes happens, the man or his wife have a particularly successful career, or a substantial inheritance, or prospect of a generous pension, there are still financial considerations of a different kind to be taken into account.

Many men who remarry and have new families simply forget the children of their first marriage, casting them aside with the divorced or deceased wife. Barbara was 38 when her father died and was heartbroken when she discovered that the will he had made when he had remarried after her mother's death, 15 years previously, simply left everything to his second wife without any mention whatsoever of her or her brother and sister. 'We naturally hadn't expected to be left a fortune,' she says. 'But to be left nothing at all, not even a chair or a picture, was devastating. My stepmother explained that when they had got married they had both made identical wills, which was all very well for her since she had no other family, but my father should never have done that.'

In this case, there were no children of the second marriage, nor had there been a divorce: both these factors, when present, make it even more likely that first families are 'forgotten' in wills. James's father was a successful builder and property developer, and James and his wife had banked – literally – on a substantial legacy when his father died. But his father had divorced and remarried, and when the long-anticipated event occurred, with James in his fifties, it transpired that everything went to the widow and children from his second marriage. James and his brother got nothing.

One fairer way of dealing with remarriage mentioned above, although it probably wouldn't have helped James because of his age, is to leave funds or property in trust for the second wife to use during her lifetime and the capital to revert to the children on her death. An older father may be mainly concerned to provide for the children of his second marriage who may well still be minors when he dies: fair enough, but his other children shouldn't be forgotten, even if he thinks he has been generous to them in his lifetime. Such thoughtlessness can embitter step-relationships quite unnecessarily after a man's death.

MORTALITY AND ILLNESS

However healthy older fathers may feel today, they wonder how things will look 'ten years from now'. Middle-aged men, even without small children, tend to look at time in a different way from when they were young: they see it in terms of years to live rather than years since birth.

Older fathers think even more about these things. They worry about the age gap of 40 or 50 years which will always separate them from their children – a gap which cannot be talked away or looked at entirely positively. How will it all turn out? they wonder. Will I ever see my grandchildren? Will I even see these children grown up?

Every so often, well-known men die in middle age leaving small children behind and the media run prominent stories suggesting that they have behaved in some way irresponsibly.

Certainly, the worst fear of many older fathers – especially those whose children are born when they are over 60 – is that they will die before their children have grown up. Undoubtedly, the risk is there and, just as certainly, the children will suffer. Some psychologists suggest that men *are* being irresponsible in having children over the age of, say, 45. But the absence of a father through divorce can cause similar problems. In fact, some research has suggested that divorce, particularly acrimonious divorce, has a worse effect on children than a father's death. It is a fact that at least a third of all children of divorced marriages completely lose touch with their father.

In one extensive US study of the impact on lower-class white children of father absence through death and absence through other causes, it was found that the child's age, sex and the reason for absence all influenced the impact on the child's academic and emotional development. But for both boys and girls, greater impairment was found when the father's absence was because of divorce, desertion or separation than it was when the father had died.

The effect of the father in the development of sex-role behaviour in both boys and girls has been studied in some detail, mainly by American researchers. The relationship between absent fathers and many personality problems – including juvenile delinquency, poor academic achievement, inability to adjust to stress and difficulty in forming stable sexual relationships – is well known.

Loss of the father through death may lead to more acute behavioural reactions in the children, but in the long term the impact may be less than in the case of divorced fathers, especially among older children. Another factor in child development when the father is absent is the attitude of the mother, and research indicates that poor school adjustment among father-absent boys was associated with their mothers' negative attitude towards their absent husbands. It is usually easier for a mother to talk positively about a husband who has died than one who has divorced or deserted her, and so the children are less likely to be affected.

Nevertheless, men (particularly) whose fathers died when they were children seem to be frequently disadvantaged. One US study found that such men continued to be very dependent on their mothers if their mother did not remarry, and only one of the ten men whose mothers did not remarry seemed to show a fair degree of independence in his own marriage.

Another study of young married men whose fathers had died before they married found that the death of the father before the age of 12 was associated with a high rate of marriage difficulty. Such men were described as immature and lacking in interpersonal competence, and their marriages were devoid of intimacy and closeness. When the husbands had lost their fathers after the age of 12, their marriage relationships were more likely to be positive.

Much of the sexual difficulty experienced by young men whose fathers had died or deserted them in childhood seems to be associated with their compulsive rejection of anything that they perceive as being related to femininity. Proving that they are not homosexual or effeminate is a major preoccupation, sometimes leading them to engage in a Don Juan pattern of behaviour. The fear of again being dominated by a female, as they were as children, contributes to their need to show off their masculinity continually by new conquests. These attributes are of course also found in sons of present but inadequate or cold fathers.

The threat of illness is another big worry. Certainly, the children of fathers who became ill or incapacitated suffer and resent it (see Chapter 6). But what evidence there is suggests that older fathers take their responsibilities very seriously, both in terms of making proper provision for death and disability through insurance, and of following healthy lifestyles and having check-ups. One American psychologist, Jerrold Lee Shapiro, has found that fathers over 40 are often prompted to take steps towards a healthier lifestyle, perhaps quitting smoking, cutting down on alcohol or giving up a dangerous hobby. 'One older father I know had been driving racing cars for years and years,' he says. 'When the baby was born, he was 41 or 42. That was it. He just gave it up.'

Because of the risks of illness and death, many men contemplating older fatherhood, particularly those over 50, may seriously worry about whether they will make adequate fathers or whether they will see their children grow up. But perhaps their fears are misplaced. As British fertility expert Professor Ian Craft, who has helped many older couples have children, points out, 'Life is a privilege, and very few people regret being born.'

It's also clear that very few older fathers, once they've taken the plunge, regret having children later in life. What they should do – and most of them seem only too aware of their responsibilities – is to take what precautions they can to reduce the risks of their becoming incapacitated or dying and to limit the impact on their children should the worst happen.

AFTERWORD

A LATE GIFT

Thomas, the youngest of my total of nine children, is only five (which is what his twin sister would also be had she lived) and was a gift to me in my sixtieth year. The next youngest graduated from Oxford this year, so the gap is some 15 years. I have assisted at all but the first of my children's births, and it never ceases to amaze me how potent and atavistic is the charge from seeing the young born.

But this last time, I realised there was also something selfish in bringing into the world a child who might not know his father for long. That is one of the pains of age, and it is an unthinking mother or father who does not take this into account. When Thomas is at university, if I am lucky, I will be 80.

It is undoubtedly true that children conceived in later life have a special and precarious position. His mother is a mere 38 now, and can be, indeed is, single-minded in her devotion to him; whereas I am of many minds, and he is both a joy and a charge.

The peculiarities of Thomas's life, however, are many. He is well aware of being a twin, and of having a sister with the angels. He is also aware of being in a generational confusion. He lives in a world populated by nephews and nieces who are something like his own age, while his true siblings must seem every bit as old as myself. Not an only child, he is one to all intents and purposes. And I no longer have the limitless energy of the young parent, nor even, always, the kindness I should have.

But as the child of an aged father, he has a kind of wisdom and balance that his siblings didn't attain until they were considerably older. The dinner table at which he grows up is populated by greybeards whom he will not know in adulthood. He will have many losses, myself among them. But I do not think that he, any more than I, would wish it otherwise. Life is a very precious gift and in return for that he can bring me back not only to the early days of his siblings, but also to the wonder of my own childhood.

The love I bear him is that much greater for being a late gift, and for my knowing that it will continue to illuminate me, should I live long enough, when my oldest are seeing their first grandchildren into this world. I suspect his brothers and sisters also feel a certain awe: that he is so young and yet enjoys such a long past and such a long future.

A Poem to My Father

Sitting silent, time the victor for once has ceased
 his fire.
Peace as I hold your hand and you hold my heart.
Looking through your old flesh, seeing both your
 spirit and your skull,
And I love them both, the wind of your spirit and
 the earth of your skull,
That was never meant to be more than a
 temporary measure,
Though never would we believe it.
For all that you have given me never have I been
 truly grateful
Until this moment.
Out of all the responsibilities that you have laid
 before me,
All are pale compared to the faith that you have in
 me.
Your love I shall forever embrace and carry with
 me,
Never losing sight of that wide right eye that
 stares at me

That looks straight in the face of my soul
For you know.
What? I'm not quite sure,
But you know and I glimpse and am fortunate
For I too wish to stare and maybe shall, striving in
     honour of you, your love and your hand.
And when it's time for home, I shall cry the tears
     of love
Knowing that the words were right and that I am
     not of you but I am from you
And I shall walk on through the night and into the
     day.
Yes father, you are right, it is sad, but if it wasn't
     sad
It wouldn't be love.

by Joe Wright, born when his father was 65
January 1990
(©Joe Wright, reproduced with permission.)

USEFUL ADDRESSES

UK

British Agencies for Adoption and Fostering
11 Southwark Street
London SE1 1RQ
Tel: 071 407 8800

British Pregnancy Advisory Service
Fertility problems and vasectomy reversal.
Austy Manor
Wooten Wawen
Solihull
West Midlands
Tel: 0564 793225

Families Need Fathers
A national support and campaigning group for non-resident
(formerly non-custodial) fathers.
134 Curtain Road
London EC2A 3AR
Tel: 071 613 5060

Family Planning Association
27 Mortimer Street
London W1N 7RJ
Tel: 071 636 7866.

Future Perfect
Careers counselling for over-forty-fives.
101 Hadleigh Road
Leigh-on-Sea
Essex SS9 2LY
Tel: 0702 72634

National Childbirth Trust
Alexandra House
Oldham Terrace
Acton
London W3 6NH
Tel: 081 992 8637.

Parent-to-Parent Information on Adoptive Services (PPIAS)
Lower Boddington
Daventry
Northamptonshire NN11 6YB
Tel: 0327 60295

Relate: National Marriage Guidance Council
Herbert Gray College
Little Church Street
Rugby
Warwickshire
Tel: 0788 573241

Stepfamily: The National Stepfamily Association
72 Willesden Lane
London NW6 7TA
Tel: 071 372 0844

Surgical Advisory Service
23 Harley Street
London W1N 1DA
Tel: 071 637 3110
Vasectomy reversal

USA

American Society of Separated and Divorced Men
575 Keep Street
Elgin
Illinois 60120
Tel: (312) 965 2200

The Fatherhood Project
Family and Work Institute
330 7th Avenue
New York
NY 10001
Tel: (212) 268 4846

Full-time Dads
PO Box 120
Cumberland
Maine 04021

ParentAGE
19 West 21 Street
New York
NY 10010-6805
Tel: (212) 924 9400
Monthly magazine for 'the new parent over 35'.

WOOM: Wives of Older Men
1029 Sycamore Avenure
Tinton Falls
New Jersey 07724-3198
Tel: (908) 747 5586
Support group

AUSTRALIA

Family Planning Australia (national)
PO Box 9026
Deakin
ACT 2600
Tel: (62) 85 1244

State Associations

FP ACT
Health Promotion Centre
Childers Street (PO Box 1317)
Canberra
ACT 2601
Tel: 06 247 3077
Fax: 06 257 5710

FP NSW
328–336 Liverpool Road
Ashfield
NSW 2131
Tel: 02 716 6099
Fax: 02 716 6164

FP NT
Shop 11, Rapid Creek Shopping Centre
Trower Road
Rapid Creek
NT 0810
Tel: 089 48 1044
Fax: 089 48 0626

FP QLD
100 Alfred Street
Fortitude Valley
QLD 4006
Tel: 07 252 5151
Fax: 07 854 1277

FP SA
17 Phillips Street
Kensington
SA 5068
Tel: 08 31 5177
Fax: 08 364 2389

FP TAS
73 Federal Street (PO Box 77)
North Hobart
TAS 7002

Tel: 002 347 200
Fax: 002 347 674

FP VIC
270 Church Street (PO Box 274)
Richmond
VIC 3121
Tel: 03 429 3500
Fax: 03 427 9987

FP WA
70 Roe Street (PO Box 141)
Northbridge
WA 6003
Tel: 09 227 6177
Fax: 09 227 6871

Canberra Family Support Service
42 Canberra Avenue
Forrest ACT 2603
Tel: 06 239 7700

Canberra One Parent Family Support
PO Box 685
Civic Square ACT 2601
Tel: 06 247 4282

Concerned Parents Group
15 Finlayson Place
Gilmore ACT 2905
Tel: 06 288 0217

Family Care Cottage
14 Ruttledge Street
Queanbeyan
NSW 2620
Tel: 06 299 1155

Lone Fathers' Association
GPO Box 492
Canberra City ACT 2601
Tel: 06 258 4216

Non-Custodial Parents Action Group
PO Box 1021
Belconnen ACT 2616

Parent and Child Support Group
PO Box 1066
Tuggeranong ACT 2901
Tel: 06 293 2919

Parent Support Service
Majura Community Centre
Rosevear Place
Dickson ACT 2601
Tel: 06 247 0519

Parents without Partners
PO Box 465
Dickson ACT 2602
Tel: 06 248 6333

FURTHER READING

Jo Boyden with UNESCO, *Families: Celebration and hope in a world of change*, Gaia Books, London, 1993.

Deborah Fowler, *A Guide to Adoption: The Other Road to Parenthood*, Optima, 1993.

Martin Francis, *Fathering for Men*, Generation Books, 1986.

Sean French (ed), *Fatherhood: Men write about fathering*, Virago, 1992.

Tony Gibson, *Love, Sex and Power in Later Life*, Freedom Press, 1992.

Jeremy Hamand, *Prostate Problems: The complete guide to their treatment*, Thorsons, 1991.

Maggie James, *Marrying an Older Man*, Piatkus Books, 1993.

Michael Lamb (ed), *The Role of the Father in Child Development*, John Wiley, New York, Revised edition, 1981.

Charlie Lewis and Margaret O'Brien (eds), *Reassessing Fatherhood: New observations on fathers and the modern family*, Sage, 1987.

G. Robina Quale, *Families in Context*, Greenwood Press, 1992.

Kate Raphael, *A Step-parent's Handbook*, Sheldon Press, 1986.

Mark Bruce Rosin, *Stepfathering: Stepfathers' advice on creating a new family*, Ballantine, New York, 1987.

Dr Christine E. Sandford, *Enjoy Sex in the Middle Years*, Optima, Revised edition, 1990.

Richard Seel, *The Uncertain Father: Exploring modern fatherhood*, Gateway Books, 1987.

Jerrold Lee Shapiro, *The Measure of a Man: Becoming the father you wish your father had been*, Delacorte Press, New York, 1993.

Edward Shorter, *The Making of the Modern Family*, Collins, 1976.

Dr Miriam Stoppard, *The 50 plus Lifeguide*, Dorling Kindersley, London, 1983.

INDEX